LOST AND FOUND *in Cuba*

A Tale of Midlife Rebellion

Jeanne Parr Lemkau

Jeanne Lemkau

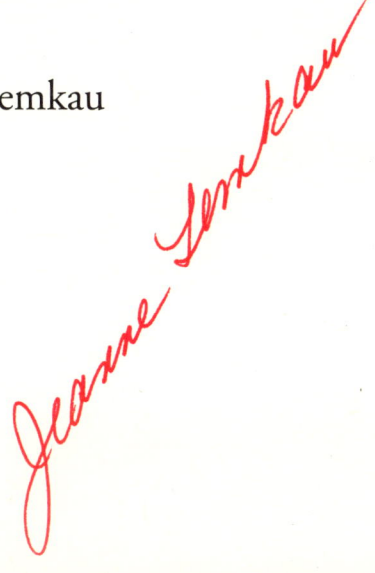

Published by Orton Road Press, Yellow Springs, Ohio

ISBN: 978-0-9844092-9-7

Cover design by GO! Creative, LLC; www.go-creative.net
Photography by Shawn Davis; sdavis707@gmail.com
Interior design by Lee Lewis Walsh, Words Plus Design; www.wordsplusdesign.com

Printed in the United States of America by Edwards Brothers, Inc., Ann Arbor, Michigan

To Karin
Joyful Adventures

acknowledgements

Writing this book has been its own journey, one that I could not have completed without a myriad of mentors, friends, and writing companions. First, I would like to acknowledge my fellow travelers and ex-Peace Corps volunteers from my first trip to Cuba in 2000. Had our shared adventure been less memorable, I might never have returned. Tom Walker was particularly helpful in facilitating my subsequent contacts with academic Cubaphiles.

I am grateful for the financial support and professional leave granted me by the Boonshoft School of Medicine of Wright State University, without which I would not have been able to travel to Cuba a second, third, fourth, or fifth time. I especially thank Mark Clasen who supported my inchoate plans, even knowing their realization might dislodge me from the institution we both served.

Special thanks to Wayne Smith for his ready counsel and for his generosity in allowing me to travel under the specific license of Johns Hopkins University. I am also grateful to Bob Schwartz for his belief in my proposed research collaboration, for his practical suggestions on approaching the *Ministerio de Salud Pública*, and for allowing me to travel under the specific humanitarian license of the DISARM Education Fund.

Two writing programs were invaluable as I worked to translate my Cuba experience to the written page. I thank the faculty of the Goucher College MFA program in creative nonfiction, most notably, Diana Hume George for her ruthless line-editing and incisive psychological probes, and Tom French for insisting that I find out the name of the dog. While I was in Havana, several fellow Goucher students helped me find my voice through lengthy email exchanges. Of these, I owe special thanks to Laronda Bowen Fruin who, lured by my writing to visit Cuba herself, gave me confidence that I might find a larger audience.

Faculty and participants of the New Directions Program of the Washington Center for Psychoanalysis were infinitely tolerant and supportive of this writing project, in spite of the fact that it didn't remotely relate to psychoanalysis. From this program, I thank graduates Gina Sangster-Hayman, Lynn Borenstein, and Nora Minnies, and faculty members Martha Dupecher, Sue Willens, Mary Crawford, Sharon Alperovitz, and Bob Winer. Heartiest thanks go to Sara Taber Mansfield and Nan Heneson for their editorial wisdom and for helping me curb my obsessive ruminations by believing in the sum of the parts.

I had the pleasure of writing retreats in two extraordinarily beautiful places; Scientists' Cliffs, Maryland, and Amherst, Virginia. Hal Rogoff and Laurie Kauffman rented me their log cabin on the cliffs of the Chesapeake Bay for weeks of solitary writing over the past five years. The cabin, built by my grandparents in the 1930s, gave me the precious opportunity to feel the presence of ancestral spirits while mentally inhabiting the two distinct geographies of Scientists' Cliffs and Havana. The Virginia Center for the Creative Arts granted me fellowships in 2008 and 2009, providing the time, space, and community that I needed to complete the manuscript.

I have benefited from the critical comments and encouragement of Carol Lachenman, Elizabeth Cohn, Mary Stukenberg, Mavis Anderson, Joy Joseph, Sara Lachenman, Diane Simpson, Susan Carpenter, Kate Cauley and Ira Bruckner. Thanks also to Paulino Velasco, *mi maestro por Skype,* for reviewing Spanish in the text.

Most importantly, I offer *mils gracias* to my family—from Chapel Hill to Yellow Springs to Woods Hole to Tokyo—for loving me whether I wrote this book or not, for celebrating my Cuba pilgrimage with me, and for the endless games of Scrabble that prepared me to become a writer: please notice the seven-letter words. My debt of gratitude is deepest to my husband Phil, who supported me when my need for adventure entailed his spending winter months alone in Ohio with only the dog for company.

To the doctors, landlords, taxi drivers, nuns, patients, and pilgrims who appear in these pages and inspired them, I offer my heartfelt thanks.

introduction

I first visited Cuba on a whim. It was 2000 and my only child was packing her bags for college when I was invited to learn about the Cuban public health system as part of an educational exchange sponsored by the National Peace Corps Association and the Friendship Force. The prospect of spending a week in the company of other former Peace Corps volunteers attracted me as much as the destination. Two years of Peace Corps service in Nicaragua during the early 1970s and half a dozen trips to Central and South America over the subsequent decades had nurtured my interest in Latin America, and as a psychologist and professor of family medicine, the trip's focus suited me. But of Cuba, I knew little more than that it was a Caribbean island that had been taken over by a revolutionary Fidel Castro when I was still learning fractions in grade school.

Weeks before the trip, a thick envelope appeared in my mailbox, stuffed with articles promising to prepare me for what our group would see, but I was too distracted by Karin's departure to do more than peruse them. When I arrived in Havana, I was an empty slate ready to be written upon by the raw experience of Cuba. During seven days of hospital and home visits, meetings with health professionals and state officials, city tours and private explorations, I tried to bring Cuba into focus, but it seemed as if I were looking through a pair of glasses with the wrong prescription. Drawing any conclusions proved to be difficult; the mix of the foreign and the familiar was too baffling. Havana had the color and verve and bustle of every other Latin American city that I knew, but the misery was missing. I saw no tar paper shacks with squalid dirt floors, no children sleeping in cardboard boxes in the streets, no emaciated babies with sad eyes, no walls topped with barbed wire and shards of broken glass to protect palatial homes. Even as I tried to make sense of what *wasn't* there, unexpected contrasts vied for my attention. Well-stocked "dollar" stores mixed with sparsely-supplied *bodegas.* Images of Che Guevara interspersed with likenesses of Abraham Lincoln. Seventeenth century houses in sun-drenched pastels stood near grotesque Russian buildings that reminded me of those I had seen in the communist Czechoslovakia I visited as a teenager.

Puzzling contradictions pervaded my view of the health system too: dilapidated hospitals but superb health statistics, universal access to medical care but serious shortages of medicines, paltry salaries but enthusiastic physicians—all within a cultural motif that, at least on the surface, emphasized the collective: *"!La revolución somos todos!"*

Although flawed and struggling, the Cuban model of health care, based on the radical notion of health as a fundamental human right, offered an alternative vision of the possible, beyond the provision of medical care based on wallet biopsy and insurance coverage with which I was more familiar. With our health care system in shambles and millions of our people without access to care, I was eager to explore more deeply Cuba's "population-based" approach to health care, one rarely covered by mainstream media at home.

Hooked on Cuba, I was determined to return. Thankfully, from this first trip, I learned just enough to write a plausible application for professional leave for the following year. I proposed to study the Cuban health care system and to conduct research on how doctors and patients coped with the effects of the embargo that blocked the import of drugs and medical supplies from the United States and from international subsidiaries of American companies.

In 2001 and 2002, I made four month-long research trips to Cuba while on leave from the medical school where I taught. As it happened, in the period prior to my sabbatical leave, I had been going through a difficult period in my personal and professional life. In heading to Havana, I was seeking my own health along with the answers to research questions.

Returning to Cuba was no trivial matter. As part of the general ban on commercial transactions with the country, citizens of the United States are forbidden by their government from travelling there; although technically, spending money and not travel itself is forbidden. The travel ban, a key component of the trade embargo that has governed U.S.-Cuba relations for half a century, was designed to squeeze the Cuban economy and provoke the collapse of the Castro regime. Two Castros and eleven American presidents later, the embargo still stands.

Exceptions to the travel ban for educational, journalistic, and humanitarian reasons have been variously allowed under different administrations, typically requiring advanced application and "specific license," a document issued to the approved traveler prior to departure. In contrast, research travel is covered by "general license," and requires no advanced application. For general license, one must comply with the requirements of the Office of Foreign Assets Control (OFAC) of the U.S. Department of the Treasury. The traveler must be a full-time professional whose travel transactions are directly related to non-commercial research, with a full work schedule in Cuba and substantial likelihood of public dissemination of findings. Under an obscure 1918 regulation that forbids "Trading with the Enemy," anyone who returns from Cuba without a specific license can be charged and fined unless they can demonstrate to immigration officials their eligibility for general license. The intimidating after-the-fact nature of this assessment has deterred many a prospective traveler.

In the nine years since I first touched down in Havana, I traveled to Cuba eight times. I sought coverage by specific license whenever possible. Other times I claimed eligibility for general license and ran the gauntlet of interrogation upon reentry. Each trip strengthened my conviction that all restrictions of travel to Cuba—and the embargo itself—should be abolished. Toward that end, proceeds from the sale of this book support the Cuba program of the Latin America Working Group Education Fund (www.lawg.org).

What follows is memoir, an account of four months in Cuba based on my recollections filtered through my current psychological understanding. I drew from detailed contemporaneous field notes and photographs in reconstructing the events and encounters herein described. My notes were only occasionally verbatim, so dialogues represent my best recall and approximation of conversations. Out of deference to all I cannot decipher about a country and culture not my own, I have chosen to err on the side of caution by altering names and minor identifying details for some individuals who appear in these pages. Otherwise, what is written here is true to my experience. Any errors of fact or understanding are mine alone.

part 1

flight

chapter 1

The seat of my chair sagged too close to the floor and allowed me neither to settle nor rise with ease. As I sat in the lobby of the Hotel Plaza in Central Havana, a tall uniformed doorman at the main entrance welcomed guests with a sweep of his arm. They streamed by me, heading eagerly toward the bar and their afternoon *mojito*s, seeking relief from the tropical heat. Graying middle-aged men, sporting straw hats and fanny packs, belched smoke from newly purchased *Cohibas* as they passed. Over the neo-classical arch that separated the lobby from the bar hung a sign that read, *"El socialismo además de justicia, es eficiencia y es calidad."* Socialism, aside from being just, is efficiency and quality. Surrounded by frothy pink and white architectural frosting, the message seemed odd.

I had just arrived. Tentatively, I reached for the old-fashioned telephone on the pedestal table next to me, a model I had only seen in movies from the forties. The receiver felt heavy and awkward when I put it to my ear and my line was connected with the hotel operator.

"Quiero hacer una llamada," I said, my voice faltering, *"Por favor."* I hadn't spoken Spanish for over a year, and then I had been in a group with a translator. Now I was on my own, and whenever I spoke, I tiptoed linguistically, unsure of what I would say or understand in a country where Spanish appeared to have neither vowels nor consonants.

The phone connection crackled. I thought the operator said that I needed to see the hotel receptionist before I could place a call. Pushing myself up from my chair, I approached the front desk jammed and jangling with tourists conversing in Spanish and German and Dutch. A cluster of cute young women in navy suits and white blouses busily attended them.

"Perdóneme," I ventured, trying to catch the eye of one of the receptionists. Should I have said *"Discúlpeme?"* I wondered, wishing I had taken the time to learn when to use these two versions of "Excuse me."

She looked my way. *"¿El teléfono?"* I asked.

"Un dólar la llamada," she replied, gesturing for me to leave a dollar and return to the table with the telephone.

I poked at the waistline of my skirt, loosening the money belt where I had stashed fifteen hundred dollars in cash, my best guess as to what I might need to live for one month in Havana. I figured on fifty dollars a day to cover lodging, transportation, and food, hopefully with enough left over for extras or emergency. I'd left credit cards at home, no good here since the embargo forbade U.S. banks to do business with Cuba. I handed the young woman a dollar and headed toward the phone. Suddenly overwhelmed by fatigue, heat, and confusion, I collapsed back into my chair.

Like the '54 Chevy I had seen from the taxi coming in from the airport, for some time I had been puttering along—with an engine held together with duct tape and a prayer, but puttering along—until this whiz-bang collision with Cuba. Now I felt all bent fender and broken headlights, stalled in the middle of a busy intersection. It was only Day One and already the reality of what I had chosen to do felt much harder than I had anticipated. How was I going to manage a full month in Havana when the simple act of making a phone call overwhelmed me?

A wave of anxiety washed over me as I thought about the grandiosity of my proposed agenda. In my request for professional leave I had promised to "study the Cuban health care system and the effects of the embargo." What I had written sounded plausible enough to elicit approval from the requisite university committee, but I'd omitted the details because I didn't have any. Like most university faculty, I had learned the stressful art of making a public commitment—to write a paper or teach a course for which I was unprepared—and then, in a fit of panic, rushing marginally legitimate delivery.

The style, albeit nerve-wracking, had boosted my productivity. But never before had I been quite this bold. I must have been in a state of wild self-delusion to think I could live up to the expectations I had generated. This was Cuba, a country more foreign than any other I had visited, a country where I knew no one and where my linguistic pretensions would be tested.

And Cuba was communist. Even if my language skills were adequate, I imagined the country was rife with secret protocols and cultural mandates that I would never be able to decipher. Dealing with my emotional insides was going to be more of a challenge than I had anticipated.

I tried to push away my fears, reminding myself that the agenda I had set for this first month was modest—to get used to Havana, immerse myself in Cuban Spanish, make initial contacts, and develop a research plan that I would carry out in future trips. "Take one day at a time," I told myself, as if I were one of my alcoholic patients. But my best attempts at cognitive therapy offered little relief, only making me feel an internal schism, as if my anxiety inhabited one house and an objective observer had moved in next door.

I fingered the satchel of papers in my lap, several pages of names, phone numbers, and addresses I had compiled in hopes that these contacts would give shape and direction to what would come next. There were names of doctors and psychologists, friends of friends, and distant nodes on the worldwide web of Cuba aficionados. Only two people on the list had I actually ever met, and those just briefly at international meetings in the United States. One was an economist turned tour organizer named Rodrigo, listed in my notes as "My Man in Havana," as if wishing would make it so. The second was a physician named Enrique.

The doctor would have to wait. I felt too shaky to approach a new colleague on the telephone in a language that reduced me to a sixth grade vocabulary. Besides, in the span of half a day and two airplane flights, I had tumbled down Maslow's hierarchy of needs; the necessity of finding shelter, food, and care eclipsed loftier aspirations. I needed a place to live that was within my budget and that would offer human contact beyond the tourist-hotel variety.

By email when I was back in Ohio, Rodrigo had assured me that he would arrange for me to stay in a *casa particular*, a private home where for twenty-six dollars a day I could live with a family and be fed "the best food in Cuba." A phone call when I reached Havana, he said, would do the trick. I read his phone number to the hotel operator.

I had a vague vision of the living situation I was hoping for. Back in the early seventies, during several months of Peace Corps training in Puerto Rico, my husband, Phil, and I had lived in the home of Anna and Carlos and their five children, surrounded by sugar cane fields and within earshot of the local cantina. Anna spoke English but only as last resort, instead patiently encouraging and correcting our Spanish baby talk. The children were our younger siblings. Anna felt like Mom, Carlos, our benevolent father.

We'd been in our early twenties. Now I was in my fifties. But with only a few hours in Havana behind me, I already felt orphaned. It didn't matter that I had *chosen* to travel to Cuba by myself or that I had a husband, daughter, and parents at home who loved me. They weren't in Havana and I felt painfully separated from the soothing familiar. Being taken in by a welcoming Cuban family was the most appealing possibility I could imagine, which was a good thing since—thanks to Rodrigo—I was about to be adopted.

From the other end of the phone Rodrigo greeted me in good English. He sensed my anxiety. *"No hay problema,"* he assured. He had arranged lodging for me with an older couple who no longer had children at home. I was to take a taxi to a certain corner in Vedado the next day. There his man Humberto would be waiting to take me to meet my new family. With a concrete plan to address my basic needs, I felt myself relax. Mustering the courage to make a second call, I gave the operator the number of the doctor.

~

When I think of Enrique now, I think of him as my Cuban brother, but I never would have guessed from our first brief encounter in the United States, how quickly our relationship would evolve from colleagues to friends to family. Our first meeting had been at a symposium on Cuban medicine. He had worn a scratchy-looking brown suit that matched his brown frizzy hair as he delivered a paper on Cuba's successful eradication of polio, smallpox, and other infectious diseases. When we spoke briefly after his presentation, he seemed uncomfortable, as if his suit were too tight. Neither of us lingered.

So I was surprised a month later when he responded to a query that I posted on a list-serve expressing interest in making contact with professionals who could help me learn more about Cuban health care. Enrique replied with his phone number and suggested that we meet to talk once I was in Havana. Given my short list of potential contacts and even shorter list of physicians, I couldn't afford to cross him off my list, even if our earlier meeting had left me with apprehensions.

When he answered the phone, I scrambled to greet him in Spanish but our conversation quickly morphed into a mix of our native tongues. He sounded pleased to hear from me and accepted my invitation to meet at the hotel café a few hours later.

Enrique strolled into the hotel looking relaxed and wearing a short-sleeved pastel *guayabera,* the typical dress-shirt of Latin America. I recognized him instantly by his fuzz of hair and European features. We shook hands. He asked about my trip and welcomed me to Cuba. In his country now, his manner was open and friendly and my initial hesitation vanished. We ordered *cervezas* in the lobby café.

More out of desperation than judgment, I trusted Enrique from our first meeting on his turf and spoke freely with him about what I hoped to accomplish in Cuba. Since I had no specific plans, I could only converse in generalities, but we quickly established common ground: we shared interests in primary care medicine; my department was family medicine and he had trained as a family physician before specializing in epidemiology; we shared research skills and a love of writing. He looked to be a few years younger than me, but the difference wasn't great. Linguistically we were well matched too. His English was about as good as my Spanish, and each of us was competent to understand but hesitant to initiate in a foreign tongue. Later, as I settled into Cuba, we settled into Spanish, punctuated by my frequent queries of *"¿Cómo se dice…?"* and his frequent provision of the words that eluded me.

I picked up the tab. We would talk more, Enrique said, once I had moved into my lodging in Vedado and acclimated.

The following afternoon, I flagged a yellow cab in front of the hotel and showed the *taxista* the address that Rodrigo had given me. It was easier than trying to say it, and I was conserving my energy.

Leaving the hotel, we turned onto Calle Neptuno and entered Central Havana. I stared out the window, taking in block after block of decayed nineteenth century buildings, huddled shoulder-to-shoulder in dust and diesel haze. The thoroughfare was congested with bicycle rickshaws, beeping taxis, and pedestrians trying to keep to the broken sidewalks. Old cars spewed their sooty fumes into the narrow street. We crossed several wide boulevards lined with grayed gritty edifices and pillared walkways and finally climbed a long hill and came to a brief stop in front of the grand stairway entrance to the University of Havana. According to my map, we were just entering Vedado, the municipality where I would be living. With Central Havana behind, more modern buildings pulled me into the twentieth century.

We passed the Habana Libre Hotel, the Hilton in its pre-revolutionary incarnation and one of the city's most prominent landmarks. An abstract mosaic in black, blue, and white decorated the front of the boxy tower. Just beyond, the taxi jerked to a stop at the main intersection of Vedado where, in front of an ice cream stand, loomed a billboard Fidel Castro in military green, his fist in the air, and his image emblazoned with the declaration, "*Against terrorism and against the war!*"

It jarred me. Without wanting to, I remembered 9/11, fresh in my memory. Two months earlier, my plane tickets had been purchased and I was in the midst of saying goodbyes to my patients when the twin towers of the World Trade Center fell. For weeks I felt like a stranger in my own body, simultaneously transfixed and repelled by the media coverage. As the world divided into sides, the idea of foreign travel began to feel both riskier and weighted with extra meaning. I considered cancelling plans but hesitated, knowing that staying home wouldn't magically protect the people I loved and not wanting to retreat in fear. Finally, knowing that I would be seen as foolish or unpatriotic by some, I decided to stay on course, spurred by the urge to leave difficulties behind and by the desire to blur an international boundary and affirm common humanity with my choice.

My taxi turned left in front of the super-sized Fidel. We traversed avenues dotted with statues and topiary, passed a movie theater named for

Charlie Chaplin, then made several more turns. Though the streets were potholed and the houses a bit scrappy, the neighborhood looked better off than Central Havana. A canopy of trees shaded the broken sidewalks, and green plants crowded each other on patios. So far so good, I thought. The driver slowed to verify the address as we neared our destination. On our right stood a mint green apartment complex, on our left, a block of adjoined one-story houses with patios. There, in front of a chicken-wire fence, a man waved us over. It was Humberto, the man who worked for Rodrigo. He was a noticeable presence, with over six feet of authority, wavy black Elvis hair, and a surplus of gold necklaces that suggested he had family in Miami.

Humberto grabbed my bags, unlocked the metal gate and led me through the patio to the wooden front door. It was almost double my height and propped open. Hearing us approach, Dulce and Norberto—my hosts—burst through the doorway in an explosion of friendly greeting, the two of them chattering loudly at once. Awash in a torrent of Spanish, I understood little.

"Me llamo Juanita," I ventured, hardly recognizing the timidity in my voice. "*Juana*" would have been more appropriate now that I was middle-aged, but the younger version seemed to be the only appellation available to me.

Norberto and Dulce pulled me into a noisy tangle of hugs and pats. The grapple of their welcome took me by pleasant surprise, evoking the physicality of Nicaraguans that I had enjoyed in my Peace Corps years. I gave myself over to their hands and arms.

"Juan—EEE—ta, Juan—EEE—ta," Norberto squealed. He was a diminutive fellow. He reached up and grabbed both of my shoulders to get a closer look, then displayed all of his teeth in a grin that seemed to hang on his cup-shaped ears. I couldn't help but laugh. Dulce tugged my arm, pulling me deeper into their cozy home.

Norberto and Dulce were five to ten years older than I was. They were physically matched only in their coloring—their skin dark honey, their eyes chocolate brown. Otherwise, they were a study in contrast. She was all curves and plumpness, generous in size and disposition; he, all muscles and angles, compacted in a tiny frame. Her voice was soft and soothing, his robust and booming as if to compensate for his stature. When he spoke to me, he loudly enunciated every syllable, as if each word were a carefully wrapped gift.

With Dulce at one elbow, Norberto the other, I was given the house tour. It was brief as their dwelling was modest, though the oversized entrance and twenty foot ceilings made it seem larger. The living room was furnished with a sofa, dark wooden chairs covered with red plastic cushions, and a television surrounded by knick-knacks. Their dining room was crowded with a table and enough chairs to accommodate a large family. The only bathroom was entered through the kitchen. To my relief they had hot water. Norberto stood on tiptoes and stretched to show me how to adjust the heater that wrapped around the showerhead.

The room that would be mine was off the living room. It was clean and tidy with all the amenities I could hope for: a good reading light, a wall mirror, an empty closet with hangers, shuttered windows that I could close at night, and even a small Soviet refrigerator that Norberto had earned by participating in state-sponsored demonstrations for the return of Elián González when the six year old had washed up on Florida shores.

That night as I collapsed onto the freshly made double bed, I knew I had found a nest I could settle into. With Norberto and Dulce I would have a secure base from which to figure out my next steps. They might not be Mom and Dad, but they would care for me.

chapter 2

If I'd had a different set of parents, Cuba wouldn't have occurred to me as an escape option. When I was five years old my mother and father unwittingly taught me that by leaving one country and living in another, I could exchange one life for an alternative one in a parallel universe. On a lazy lemonade of a summer afternoon, I stood knee high at my mother's side at a family gathering as she exclaimed to my aunt, "Jeannie thinks that when I say we are going *out* of the country, we are going *to* the country!" The two laughed at my expense. I resolved not to be the brunt of such adult amusement. I would figure out what it was to go "out of the country." And I did, shortly thereafter, when my father took professional leave from his university and our family boarded an ocean liner and sailed to England.

To my child eyes and ears, everything was different on the other side of the Atlantic. Lacking central heat, our Cambridge house was so frigid that we wore mittens at the breakfast table. Gone was the silver-finned Pontiac that my dad used to drive on Sunday outings; now I sat on the back of my mother's bicycle, my arms tight around her waist. Dad no longer mowed the grass; an old troll trimmed our lawn on his knees with hand clippers. My first grade teacher in the British public school insisted that I sing new words—"God Save the Queen"—to the tune of "My Country 'Tis of Thee." Expunge. Replace. Patriotisms were interchangeable.

It was hard to cope with so much change. When my teacher smacked my knuckles with a ruler for playing in puddles during recess, I missed the kindness of my kindergarten teacher in Pittsburgh. Once when my parents hopped the English Channel to vacation in Paris, my brother and sister and I were left at the mercy of an Irish babysitter who fed us nothing but potatoes for a week. And when I went to the garden to pick gooseberries for my mother, nettles surprised me, stinging like jellyfish. New traumas and new pleasures taught me to appreciate the startle of fresh geography. Going "out of the country" altered everything.

England was the first of several extended trips abroad that came to define family life, trips where I observed my father swept up in the whirl of international quantum chemistry. Invited to participate in a scientific interchange in communist Hungary, Dad didn't hesitate to say yes or to take us along. "Science has no international borders," he announced, as if this were another axiom of his discipline, and the Iron Curtain dissipated into feathers.

Mom was Dad's equal in boldness, cultivating adventures for the rest of us while he was professorially occupied. She had a penchant for talking to strangers, who inevitably responded to her sociability with invitations. Before we figured out how she had done it this time, we would be examining torpedoes on an air craft carrier or sharing roasted chestnuts with a peasant family in a noisy slum in Naples. Once she took us to watch dog races. There wasn't another woman or child in the bleachers. Chorused with cat calls, my mother was undaunted as we children watched the spectacle, transfixed by the greyhounds speeding after the rabbit bait.

To Mom and Dad there were no places off limits to travel, no options too frightening to consider. I learned to ride the ridge between apprehension and adventure within the safety of their care. So when I told my parents that I planned to return to Cuba during my academic sabbatical, they took it in stride, perhaps reminded of their own risky ventures.

~

During my last days in Ohio before taking leave, I developed an acute aversion to going to work. Each morning as my key clicked into my office door, I knew that no matter what awaited me on the other side, the day would have the aesthetic appeal of instant coffee in a paper cup.

My office at the medical school had no windows, and I had been looking at the same four walls for a quarter of a century. I had joined the faculty as a young psychologist, hired to teach medical students and residents. I helped fledgling physicians refine their communication skills, reflect on their impact on patients, and learn to diagnose and manage the variety of psychological problems that prompt patients to see doctors. Mine was a position that others might envy— a secure and well-paying job that enabled Phil and me to live in a progressive and family-friendly college town.

In the early years, the challenges of the job propelled me from graduate student to professional, and the medical world enticed me as much as any foreign culture. By the time the novelty of the job wore off, our daughter Karin had arrived, and the demands of work and family left me with neither time nor energy to think deeply about meaning and direction. For years I dutifully complied with the expectations of my position. In the world of "publish or perish," I published. When asked to serve on committees, I served. When asked to teach, I taught. I saw psychotherapy patients too, always what I found most satisfying and a welcome diversion from the rest. I accepted as given the tension in my shoulders.

Obligations accumulated, meetings multiplied, and pleasures dwindled. But being a good rule follower and too focused to consider alternatives, I kept climbing the rungs of the academic ladder. By the time I reached my goal of becoming a full professor— like my father and grandfather before me—I liked only the *idea* of my job.

I had learned academic culture around the family dinner table and had been drawn by the prospect of earning a living with my mind, a life of reading books, teaching eager students, and working with colleagues of titillating intellect. Reality had fallen short, and in negotiating the university terrain I had slipped into a quagmire of burdensome expectations and responsibilities.

Flailing, I applied for federal funding to conduct a research study on how to get family physicians to refer more women for mammograms. I hoped the new project would revitalize me, but landing the grant catapulted me into a fresh predicament. Couldn't I bring in more money, I was asked, "perhaps a million dollars a year if you wanted to?" My soul needed other sustenance, but I suppressed that awareness and fell back into the familiar pattern of striving for my father's elusive approval, projected onto the screen of my department chair, himself desperate to please his father, the dean, by bringing in research dollars to replace the ones lost to a shrinking state budget. The dynamic of children striving to be good for their surrogate fathers seemed to extend all the way up to God.

I was invited to meetings with other funded researchers at the medical school. All but two of us were men. The Big Boys bantered about the sizes of their federal grants as if they corresponded with their anatomical endowments. I looked at my empty lap, pondering how in heaven's name I had gotten myself into this conundrum of success.

More and more of my time was spent in the box of my office staring into the box of my computer, writing grant applications on subjects that didn't inspire me, with colleagues I didn't especially respect. Meaning dissolved into the pixels of my computer screen. I suppressed urges to scream during faculty meetings, made jokes about existential ennui, and played and replayed Bob Dylan singing, "It's not dark yet but it's getting there." Mine was the angst of privilege, but it was fierce and unrelenting nonetheless.

My body started to protest. I dragged myself to work feeling achy and fatigued, painful joints catching me unawares. Dry eyes made my computer screen blur. For several months, doctors queried my symptoms and drew blood. In the end, rheumatology claimed me and I was diagnosed with Sjogren's disease, an autoimmune first cousin of lupus that attacks the body's lubricating system. In brilliant echo of my professional life, my body was drying up.

I struggled and lost sleep. Eye drops and medicine bottles mixed with pens and paperclips in my desk drawer. The need to manage symptoms punctured my residual illusions of youth. The doctor assured me the disease would stabilize, that it wouldn't kill me and I would learn to adjust. Easy for him to say, I thought, hot tears stinging my arid eyes. Life suddenly seemed finite. I felt like a cliché of middle-age. When a form arrived in my university mailbox asking me to document how I was spending my time, I froze, unable to fabricate percentages and categories in the face of larger questions posed by the very existence of such forms. What percentage of my working day did I spend on "departmental research?" What about "administration" or "instruction?" I wanted spaces for "deeply meaningful personal activity" or "joyful exploration," or even "return to health," though I had little that would fall into such categories.

With time I could no longer keep from asphyxiating by focusing on the work hours I most enjoyed, when I saw my psychotherapy patients. Only physical escape and the sight of trees and sky seemed to help.

I started taking mid-morning breaks away from my office. At a local café I noticed a bunch of old men—some familiar, some not—in animated discussion over their coffee cups, huddling so closely around a table that their elbows touched. Not sure if a woman would be welcome, I approached gingerly. "Might I join you?" I asked. "Please do," one of them replied. "We're not a men's group. It's just that women don't seem to want to join us." They pulled another chair into their tight circle.

Coffee with the guys at the Emporium became my escape from the loneliness of work. There were half a dozen regulars. Jim, a retired physician who had practiced in Haiti in his youth, became my role model for not growing more conservative with age. Leon, an elderly actor, was loud, flirtatious, and full of hyperbole. Clyde, the "Spock" of the group, was more knowledgeable about bio-terrorism than any of us wanted to be. And gentle Bill, a retired English professor, struggled with serious illness to join us each day. Often a muffin splayed open on the table supplemented our communal sipping.

Bill insisted on having a dictionary on hand to settle linguistic debates. He brought in a well-worn red one, threaded a chain through the binding and nailed it to a nearby counter. And it was Bill who offered to mentor me when I told him that I was interested in creative writing, as if he knew I needed help clearing a path to the next stage of my life.

My mid-morning coffee breaks became more frequent, though they only offered a temporary fix. While I didn't want to relinquish the perks of my profession—the autonomy, the cushy salary, the health insurance—I longed for the simplicity of a life unfettered by committee meetings, health worries, grant deadlines, and work I no longer wanted to do. In the deepest parts of myself, I knew that antidepressants and the status quo were not the answer. If I were to keep from imploding, I couldn't continue to obediently trudge in the habitual grooves that had become my life.

I would go back to Cuba. As soon as the idea occurred to me, it felt right—or at least as compelling as any other impulse driven by desperation. Generating a research rational to justify professional leave was within my repertoire and an appealing option, since I had felt alive and even inspired during the health tour of Cuba the previous year. With the prospect of a Cuba adventure on the horizon, I could feel blood pulsing through my veins again.

Communist Cuba was an odd destination for someone yearning to escape a too constricted life. But at some subterranean level, it was the perfect match—not that I was conscious of this at the time. I needed to grapple with a foreign country that was officially off limits, frozen in conflict with my own, and riddled with rules. Even the presence of a Major Paternal Authority Figure was auspicious. In Cuba, I could symbolically reenact and rework thinly veiled adolescent struggles for autonomy, and maybe claim an expanded sense of future possibility.

Phil endorsed my plans without needing a lot of details. After all, Karin was safely ensconced in college, and he had witnessed my struggles with work and health enough to appreciate my restlessness. I think he preferred the prospect of lively emails from Havana to another dark winter with me tearfully looking out the kitchen window. As a concession to our marriage, I decided to divide my travel into four trips, each a month long with time at home in between. If by heading to Havana I also yearned to loosen the tethers to family, this was beyond what I could have articulated then.

chapter 3

From the far end of the house I could hear the murmur of voices and the clink of dishes. I took a deep breath, aware that I was about to leave the world of my private thoughts and plummet once again off the precipice of the familiar. The moment I opened the bedroom door, Dulce called. *"Buenos días, Juanita ¿Cómo amaneciste?"* How did you rise? She spoke loudly as if that would help me understand. My rudimentary Spanish intact, I responded in kind, hesitating but then copying her use of the informal *"tú."*

"¿Café?" Dulce asked cheerfully. She extended her hand to offer me a steaming *cafecito* in a shiny black cup.

Still standing in my nightgown and robe, I put the cup to my lips. The brew was strong and sweet. Dulce patted my arm and motioned for me to follow her to the kitchen, where a pretty thirtyish woman with glossy patent-leather hair leaned over a frying pan on the stove, her long locks barely missing the oil. "This is Maela," Dulce said. "She will be cooking breakfast and dinner for you. She works for Rodrigo." I wondered why Dulce wasn't fixing me meals, but hesitated to ask.

Maela and I smiled at each other and exchanged *mucho gustos.* Dulce nodded at the cup in my hand. *"¿Ya?"* Done yet? Her gesture suggested that I should already be finished. I gulped and handed her the cup. I would learn that Cubans downed coffee like shots of hard liquor. Only foreigners sipped.

I excused myself to use the bathroom, feeling awkward with its proximity to the stove. The insubstantial door did nothing to muffle the sound of their chatter, and I could hear the sizzle of oil and smell eggs frying as I brushed my teeth. It felt too close. *Get used to it,* I told myself, then reemerged to the kitchen.

"*¿Y Norberto?*" I asked, watching Maela set the table for one. "*Ya salió,*" Dulce replied. He had left for work at seven. She had prepared his breakfast and eaten with him before Maela arrived. Apparently Norberto and I each had our own cook—strange, I thought—but as Maela served me a ham omelet, a generous heap of papaya with lime, and the requisite *café con leche,* I considered it an arrangement I could live with.

I figured that I would spend several days exploring Havana by myself, a choice that was easy to justify; I needed to get oriented, and walking the city would allow me to settle into the language in brief spurts of interaction with little demand. Of course, this plan also served to keep my fears at bay, fears about how and when and with whom I would actually accomplish my proclaimed research agenda. Walking as procrastination was a skill I would perfect.

After breakfast I retreated to my room and gathered provisions for the day: a guidebook with a map of Havana, a hat to protect my pale skin from the sun, a pared-down version of what I carried in my purse at home, a small black notebook, and about fifty dollars. Dulce had assured me that I could leave whatever I wanted, including money, safely in my room. I converted the Elian Gonzalez refrigerator into my "bank" and wrapped all but a few dollars of the $1500 in a plastic bag, then put it in the freezer. For peace of mind, I pretended that it was locked. With my hat tied under my chin, a knapsack on my back, and sturdy walking shoes peeking out from under my long skirt, I was ready.

I was headed for the front door when Dulce's voice stopped me. *"Espera un momentico. ¡Voy contigo!"* Alas, she wanted to go with me: so much for being on my own. She insisted—albeit with cheerful benevolence—on accompanying me. She wanted to show me how to use the bus. I felt like a kindergartener on the first day of school as Dulce walked me several blocks to the stop on Calle 23 and pushed forty *centavos* into my hand. To ride on *la guagua* required pesos not dollars, she explained, giving me my first lesson in switching between currencies.

A crowd was gathered at the stop. *"¿El último?"* Dulce called, as we approached, determining who had arrived just before us. A woman nodded and we took a place near her. When the bus arrived, I discovered that the line was more hypothetical than real as everyone pushed toward the open door. I hoped Dulce would stay behind, but when I climbed onto the bus, she too squeezed in. How and when I could emancipate myself from her care was unclear. She pointed to an empty seat for me, and stood nearby amidst a tight press of passengers. Across the aisle, a man in clean casual dress with hair still damp from his morning bath gave up his seat to a pregnant woman.

We passed several miles of drab and worn buildings that may have been modern and new when Castro ousted Batista. It took fifteen minutes of crowded jostling before we arrived at La Rampa, where Calle 23 crosses Calle L and slopes down to the famous sea wall of the Malecón. This intersection, with ice cream stand on one corner and the Yara movie theater on another, was the heart of modern Havana. It would become very familiar to me when I began to plan research and needed the approval of the nearby *Ministerio de Salud Pública.*

The bus jerked to a stop and Dulce and I stepped onto the sidewalk. It crossed my mind that she might follow me all day if I didn't assert myself. She was kind and wanted to help me, and I didn't want to hurt her feelings. Still, I hungered to be by myself, with no one's needs to attend to but my own. Mustering resolve, I thanked her as effusively as my Spanish allowed and insisted that I would be fine. Reluctantly, she left me on the corner to continue my explorations on foot while she took another bus home—but not before warning me to hold on tight to my knapsack and to remember the number of the bus for my return. I waved to her, turned, and strode eagerly toward the thick expanse of dust-colored buildings that marked Central Havana.

In those early days in Cuba, I learned Havana with my feet, starting and ending my explorations on public transportation. Dulce continued to coach me on the nuances of getting around economically. Usually I began each expedition at the bus stop on Calle 23. There I assumed my place in the unfolding drama as each of us on the crowded curb surveyed the buses, taxis, and private vehicles whizzing by and weighed our options according to the supply and demand of the moment and whether we were carrying pesos or dollars, in a hurry or willing to wait. It looked like a free-market economy.

Once, emboldened by example, I tried hitch-hiking, enigmatically called traveling *"por botella"*—by bottle. An orthopedic surgeon on his way home from a shift in the operating room responded to my wave, pleased to pick me up for the few dollars I offered. Young women in body-hugging dress had the edge with this mode of transport, readily scooped up by alert young men on motor scooters.

When Dulce saw me don my hat before leaving one morning, she frowned, warning me that it marked me as a foreigner. She thought I should be taking the cheap peso cabs for Cubans whenever I could. Toward that end, she advised me to stuff my hat out of sight and keep as quiet as possible. The thought that—with Scandinavian features and Nicaraguan Spanish—I could ever pass as Cuban struck me as ludicrous. Still I was touched by the vigor with which—in the service of economy—she pursued the task, as if she had already concluded that I was Cuban and just had to convince everyone else.

In fact, although I'm sure I was never mistaken for a native, I never had trouble flagging down a *colectivo.* I learned that if I didn't have the standard fare of ten pesos—about forty cents—a dollar bill was welcomed, my gesture of solidarity with the driver who put himself at risk for a fine when he picked up the likes of me. I came to love riding in these ancient *maquinas* with their vibrant paint jobs, liquid silver fenders, and reconstructed dashboards. Bumping along in a '55 Pontiac cheek to jowl with a carload of *compañeros* and no shock absorbers, I felt more like human cargo than either *norteamericana* or Cuban. There was comfort in the blur.

After being dropped close to the older parts of the city, I would spend hours walking back and forth through the centuries, from the 1700s of Old Havana to the 1800s of Central Havana and the twentieth century of Vedado. Each day was exhausting and exhilarating. The warmth of the morning quickly intensified with the blaze of the sun and by noon, shade was hard to find, especially in Central Havana, devoid of trees. I didn't mind the heat, my dry eyes preferring the steam of the tropics to the icy cold of an Ohio winter. My ability to walk for miles in the baking sun reassured me that at fifty-three I still had lots of vitality left, chronic illness be damned. In Havana threats to my health felt less internal and more environmental. To safely maneuver broken curbs, pot-holes, and buildings in their last days of defying gravity required constant looking, listening, and testing terra firma. Sometimes I had to simultaneously watch my feet to avoid landing in a ditch and scan overhead to guard against a drench of laundry water cascading from a second-story balcony. The imperative to maintain vigilance rooted me in the present, trumping my Calvinist propensity to think about the future and getting things done.

Each day I ventured forth alone in ever-widening circles—into the world of dollar stores, cigar hustlers, and housewives picking through yucca and sweet potatoes in farmers' markets. I wandered among dilapidated buildings supported with scaffolds and hovering over their less fortunate neighbors, now heaps of rubble. I passed grey-haired European men walking hand-in-hand with halter-topped adolescent *jineteras* who "jockeyed" them in pursuit of cash. Children in gold pinafores and crisp white shirts scampered by on their way to school. Men tinkered with car parts and refilled cigarette lighters in doorways along the street. Under the laurel trees of the Parque Central, I stopped to listen to a mayhem of men raucously laughing and gesticulating with their arms, and picked through the slurry of their words to figure out that they were talking *pelota*—baseball.

Havana exploded with sound from dawn until dusk and beyond, with the clanging crews of construction and deconstruction, the musical rhythms of rumbas and sambas, and the screech of people calling to each other at high volume. Any quiet conversation took place against this din. I quickly learned that the clarity of Norberto's speech was a complete anomaly. Everyone else seemed keen to delete syllables and break road rules in pursuit of linguistic speed.

Adding to the challenges of heat, noise, and language was the necessity of learning to deal with two economies and three currencies. Both Cuban pesos and dollars were used, along with *convertible*, a hybrid coin used interchangeably with American dollars but having no value off the island. It reminded me of Monopoly money. Some purchases required pesos; others, dollars. Not knowing if I would want a four peso ice cream on the street or a two dollar cup of coffee in a hotel café, I learned to be prepared for all contingencies, but my money belt didn't have enough pockets to keep three currencies separate, so three-peso Che coins consorted uneasily with George Washington quarters.

Always on these excursions there was noise and heat, often the hot soot of diesel in the air, and sometimes, utter surprise. One morning as I stood on the curb waiting to cross a congested Calle L, I was approached by a lovely little girl with long black braids and a sky-blue dress. She was perhaps seven or eight years old and looked up at me with plaintive dark brown eyes.

"Would you accompany me across the street?" she asked in Spanish, apparently assuming that I would understand.

"¿Sí, cómo no?" I said. Yes, of course.

She reached up and took my hand. We waited for a break in the traffic and crossed. Safely on the other side, she looked up at me, her curious eyes meeting mine. She smiled brightly and, with a *muchas gracias*, scurried on her way. I was stunned by the beauty of the moment, so unexpected, better than prayer. I felt the echo of her blessing the rest of the day.

Walking was an elixir, the perfect antidote for years of office confinement and joyless striving. I had exchanged my closed-in office for views in all directions, my jammed work calendar for time off the clock, a village of four thousand where my face was recognized for a city of over two million where I could savor anonymity. No one knew where I was. I had no cell phone. I was off the grid. I felt blissfully distant from the expectations of others, free to let my thoughts meander along with the rest of me. My sense of spontaneity had shriveled from disuse, but began to expand into the space created by days without schedule. Not even the omnipresent fumes kept me from feeling that I could breathe more deeply than I had in years.

~

Distances in Havana were daunting, and I readily succumbed to opportunities that promised rest and conversation. Once as I was making my way through a run-down area of Central Havana, I stumbled upon a beauty shop bustling with local women. I peered in through a broken plate-glass window held together with brown tape. Salón Ilusión looked as worn out as the neighborhood and nothing like the hotel salons that catered to tourists.

I read the posted list of services: "Manicure, pedicure, head massage, body massage, facial acupuncture, body acupuncture." I inquired and discovered that yes, though it was a state-run facility, they could serve me. Getting the works would cost 18 pesos, less than one dollar. Incredulous, I asked a second time, unsure the beautician had understood me. Was that eighteen pesos for each service or for all? *"Por todo,"* she assured. I was contemplating a complete overhaul until she mentioned that the *masajista* wasn't in. Then a survey of the sanitary conditions gave me second thoughts about becoming an acupuncture initiate. I decided to opt for the manicure and pedicure for eight and a half pesos.

My manicurist was Angela, a woman in her early forties with curly brown hair and a blotch of bleached blond in the front. Her supplies were minimal: a worn plastic pan that could accommodate one foot at a time, a small table and a few tools. The towel that she used for everything looked as though it had been. She cleaned her instruments with a puff of cotton dipped in a substance I didn't recognize but which made me think of diseases that could be transmitted with a nip of the cuticle. Her selection of polishes was limited and heavy on metallic pinks. She was emphatic about her color preferences for me, and I decided that, for the thirty cents this would cost, she could do anything she wanted with my fingers and toes.

We talked as she washed, clipped, and polished; I pressed to learn a bit about her life. She was paid a hundred and eleven pesos a month, less than five dollars, at the rate of twenty-nine *centavos* a day when she met her daily quota of 25 services. She commuted to work an hour each way on a *camello*, one of the musty-colored buses with humped roofs designed for mass transportation when the demise of the Soviet Union left the country short of fuel. She said that she worked for tips and for the paltry state pension that her years of work would bring. Whenever she spoke, her hands stopped moving, and I worried that she might be working too slowly to meet her daily quota.

Our conversation was rolling right along when I ventured to ask if life in Cuba was getting better or worse. The question erased her light manner. She drew back. *"No me meto en la política,"* she said firmly. I don't get myself into politics. "My life is *here.*" We fell silent. I retreated to what I hoped was safer ground. How was her family doctor, I asked casually, thinking for a moment about health care and my research. I knew that all Cubans had access to a doctor and nurse team that lived in their neighborhood.

"I'm very healthy," she said. "I rarely go to the *consultorio*, but my doctor visits me at home to do a Pap smear and a pelvic exam whenever I'm due." I was trying to imagine the scene when she added, "But the doctors change often. Just when you get to know them, they leave. It's that way everywhere. I don't know why."

A woman waiting to get her nails done joined our conversation. Angela told us both about her recent trip to the hospital for the removal of a cyst. "There, with my own ears," she said, "I heard a doctor tell a patient that he would not attend her unless she gifted him with cigarettes or rum. *¡Imaginase!*"

She continued, directing her words at the other woman. "Of course if I were in similar circumstances, I would try to give the doctor *something*—maybe a flower or a bottle of cologne—but never in response to such insolence." The conversation gave me a smidgeon of satisfaction; I had elicited details germane to my professional interests.

Angela, eager to correct my speech, took pleasure in my mispronunciations and seemed not to understand me even when I thought I was speaking well. She asked whether I would return again to Cuba and I told her that I would—to pursue my interest in health care, but that I might eventually want to come back as a writer.

"Just come as a *tourist* and write," she said. "If you say you are a writer, they'll worry that you will come and then go home and drop a bomb there." She paused. "Just an expression," she added. Then she made me repeat the word for writer several times "es—cri—***to***—ra, es—cri—***to***—ra," and laughed until my pronunciation of the vowels met her standard.

I paid the bill in pesos and handed Angela a dollar. Her grin plumped the apples of her cheeks. "Come back, soon," she called, as I headed back to the street.

~

Late each afternoon when the bleached-out pastels of Central Havana took on a dusky orange glow and my energies were utterly spent, I made my way home, ambivalent to relinquish my freedom for the haven of Norberto and Dulce's care. Sometimes, bone-weary, I surrendered to a pricey dollars-only cab. Lest I be found shamelessly extravagant and a poor student of Dulce's teaching, I would ask to be left a block from home so I could arrive on foot.

When my surrogate parents heard me unlatch the front gate, they would rush to greet me. Norberto would put his hands on my shoulders and kiss my cheek. "Jua—nee—ta, how ahr yooooo?" he would hoot in my ear. And if Dulce was nearby, he would add, "I hab to-oo lubs," reaching out to grab her too.

My room always looked pristine when I returned. No matter how well I thought I had made my bed before I left in the morning, Dulce would tidy it to an even higher domestic standard by the time I reappeared at the end of the day. Whichever shoes were not on my feet when I left would be freshly scrubbed while I was away. I was cared for even in my absence.

chapter 4

Everyday I struggled to decipher street chatter, initiate conversations with strangers, and hold my own in conversations with Norberto, Dulce, and Enrique. I studied grammar books and read *Granma,* the state newspaper, with a bilingual dictionary at my side. Each foray into the babble of Cuban Spanish was fueled by a synergy of fear and boldness and paid for with fatigue. I began to realize that achieving fluency in this corner of the Hispanic world would be no small feat, much more difficult than I had previously allowed myself to imagine. *Cubanismos* abounded, and verbs whose tenses were accessible to me when I woke in the morning disappeared into the vapor by midday, when I would find myself in mid-sentence, teetering at the end of a plank about to fall into treacherous waters. By sundown, my tongue fumbled even when I knew the right words. Often I didn't.

While I could produce intelligible Spanish most of the time, understanding what came my way was often impossible. If a *taxista* was shy a few teeth or came from one of the eastern provinces, I was reduced to polite nods and grunts.

"Is there a Spanish word for speaking badly?" I asked Norberto one evening.

"*Chapurreada,*" he replied, showing a glimmer of appreciation for my question. He hesitated. "Sometimes you speak a bit *chapurreada,*" he ventured, stating the obvious.

"Chapurreada," I repeated. I liked the word, although it was hard for me to get the verbal running start that I needed to roll the Rs. Still I didn't want it to describe me and I needed to become more proficient. So I called my man in Havana, Rodrigo. For five dollars a day, he assured, he could send two university students to the house each morning to tutor me for an hour.

The next day, I'd barely finished breakfast when a gorgeous young woman with piercing dark eyes arrived with a friendly rail of a fellow at her side: my tutors, Sarán and Henri. They usually taught folks who spoke little Spanish, while I'd been speaking in fits and starts for thirty years. Nevertheless they embraced the challenge of figuring out how to help.

Three or four times a week, the three of us sat in a triangle of rocking chairs on the front patio. They were an amiable pair and a pleasure to look at, Sarán in her off-the-shoulder blouses and pulled-back hair; Henri, impish and gaunt, all elbows and knees like a praying mantis. Dulce served *cafecitos* as Henri engaged me in conversation and Sarán took notes and then drilled me on my errors. Then they would switch roles. I wasn't the professor here, but the student of masterful teachers, and I reveled in the luxury.

Your Rs need work, they said, addressing a longstanding problem. I wasn't rolling the ones that needed to roll. Competing with the street noise, I repeated after them the pronunciation drills they had learned as children in school,

Erre con erre cigarro
Erre con erre carril
Rápido corren los carros
Por la línea del ferrocarril.

We laughed as I earnestly garbled the verses. Over several days with Henri and Sarán cheering me on, my Rrs lengthened and rolled. My verbs improved, and whenever I correctly rounded the corner of a pluperfect subjunctive or used a *Cubanismo* that I had heard on the street, they nodded and smiled approvingly.

Our conversations gave me confidence that I understood the gist of what was said even when I couldn't translate word for word. Their reassurance was as helpful as their drills.

As the days passed, our conversations became more personal. Henri and Sarán wanted to sate their curiosity about how things worked in the United States as much as I wanted to sate mine about Cuba. "How is medical care paid for in the United States?" Henri asked. I tried my best to explain health insurance. "You get it through your employment," I explained, as if this made sense.

"But what if someone can't work because they are very sick?" Surán puzzled. Barely in their twenties, neither of them had known any place other than Castro's Cuba. They assumed access to free medical care as a fundamental human right. My vocabulary was suddenly inadequate to explain Medicaid, Cobra benefits or Medicare, or how people cope when they fall through the cracks of our health care system. I heard myself as if from afar, sounding defensive about aspects of life in the United States that I would readily criticize at home, surprised when remnants of latent patriotism were stirred by mere requests for clarification.

~

Norberto and Dulce's house was the center for neighborhood social life, thanks to Dulce's caretaking, Norberto's effusive nature, and the fact that, unlike their neighbors, they had a telephone. In the evenings, adolescent girls in tight pants, skimpy tops, and eye makeup would stop by, dangling cigarettes and giggling while they talked to their friends. Nieces and nephews, cousins, and Dulce's grown children from an earlier marriage would stop by to chat or catch *El Comandante* Fidel on the evening news. Sometimes Norberto would curl up on the sofa with his head in Dulce's lap, and they would watch a Hollywood movie on state television. Once it was *Silence of the Lambs* dubbed in Spanish.

Coffee—thick, dark, and delicious—provided continuity to the life of the household. Dulce's morning offering consisted of two cups; always black coffee upon rising, then *café con leche* with breakfast. She prided herself in always being prepared to make another pot when someone stopped by. I found comfort in the currency of coffee, although the sweetness of the Cuban brew—the result of centuries of abundant sugar cane—took some getting used to. Whether in Cuba or at home, the ritual of coffee shared seemed to dissipate boundaries, open up relationships, and soften differences of age, nationality, and custom. Often, when a *cafecito* appeared, I would think of the guys sipping coffee at my local café at home.

It was over coffee that Dulce disclosed details of the complex relationship between Rodrigo and their household. Of the twenty-six dollars daily that I paid Rodrigo, she and Norberto received eight, thereby supplementing Norberto's peso income—the equivalent of $14 a month—with hard currency dollars. Rodrigo gave a small amount to Maela for cooking and Humberto for managing the arrangement, then pocketed what remained. Since Dulce and Norberto did not have the license required to legally rent a room, they depended on Rodrigo to discretely bring them the occasional boarder and were hostage to his terms. I squirmed with the new knowledge that my rental was of the under-the-table variety.

Dulce never quite adjusted to having someone else in her kitchen and frequently mentioned that she would prefer to cook for me herself. For my part, I felt guilty and self-indulgent when Maela served me hearty portions and more meat than I ever saw on the plates Dulce prepared for herself and Norberto.

Norberto took such pleasure in conversing and such care to speak clearly that I loved talking with him. He was so quick to articulate a *Fidelista* worldview that I began to wonder if he secretly held a different perspective, one he couldn't safely share and about which I shouldn't ask. One evening our conversation drifted toward religion. Was he Catholic? I asked. "*¿Sí, cómo no?*" he replied. Then his eyes misted as he recalled the visit of the Pope in 1998 and seeing *El Comandante* and *El Papa* together in Revolution Plaza. Prior to that pivotal event, he explained, he had guarded his Catholicism privately. With the Pope's visit, he felt the disparate parts of himself unite and became emboldened to be more public with this newfound identity.

"I am Catholic. I am revolutionary. I am FIDELISTA!" he boomed, tapping his small fists to his small chest. Then, his tone serious, he added, "And Fidel is TEN times as intelligent as *your* president. We should all surrender to him."

As if he had not made himself utterly clear, he grinned and pointed to the ceiling.

"¡Fidel —" he jabbed the air, *"—es Dios!"* I would have poked fun had he sounded less sincere.

Once, as I was finishing another of Maela's generous meals, I asked Norberto and Dulce to explain how food rationing worked. Dulce opened a drawer, removed a small booklet and pointed to a grid of dates and notations of supplies she had received. Monthly, each person was allotted six pounds of rice, a pound and quarter of beans, three pounds of white sugar, two pounds of brown sugar, a half a pound of oil, a quarter pound of salt, and—twice a month—a pound of chicken or a half pound of beef or beef/soy mix. For personal use, each adult also received a tube of toothpaste and two bars of soap, one for bathing and one for washing clothes.

Food was just one of the government subsidies available to all, Norberto explained. Housing and utilities were heavily subsidized. No one paid for either medical or dental care. They had to be frugal but were at no risk of becoming homeless or hungry. Dulce picked up the family rations at a neighborhood *bodega* every week. Then, as they could afford, they supplemented this basic *canasta* with fruits and vegetables purchased with pesos at farmers' markets. Rarely, they bought special food and soap items at "dollar stores" where prices were high and pesos were not accepted. Often they had no dollars. There were food shortages, Norberto acknowledged, but the empty shelves at grocery stores were not Fidel's fault.

"Since *el triunfo de la revolución* Fidel wanted to be in charge of everything. Therefore he assumed the responsibility of providing people with what they needed. When you see that there is little in the stores, don't think it is because Fidel doesn't want us to have things. He works very hard for us and it is the best he can do, given *el bloqueo.*"

Yes, I thought, *Fidel es Dios.*

I could have just settled into the pleasures of exploring Havana by day and sharing Dulce and Norberto's company by night, if not for the nag of conscience. I knew it was time to get to work. Whereas this month I was covered by the specific license of a university interested in my research prospects, unless I became fully engaged in research, I wouldn't have legitimate reason to make future trips either on that license or on general license, and I had no intention of changing my plans. I was feeling better in Havana than I had felt in months: I needed the promise of more time and would play by the rules to get it.

With Dulce's encouragement, I called Enrique and invited him to visit. When my guest arrived, I offered him my hand, which he shook. I felt ill at ease. The typical greeting I had observed between Cubans was more intimate—a kiss on one cheek or two, often with hands on shoulders or at least brushing arms. While I enjoyed the sensuality of Latin *saludos* and *despedidas* and easily fell into kisses and hugs with Dulce and Norberto, with Enrique I wanted to clearly establish a professional relationship. I just had no idea where to draw the lines.

We sat in the red plastic chairs in the *sala.* Dulce appeared with coffee on a tray. Enrique downed his with a jolt. Shifting between Spanish and English, we circled and discarded various possibilities for collaboration until we tentatively settled on one that appealed to us both. We would design a study to learn about how family physicians working in Havana neighborhoods managed to care for their patients in the face of the drug scarcities that resulted from the U.S. embargo. We would work on the details later, he suggested, and I should stop by his house anytime.

I liked this man. He had kind and intelligent eyes and the beginnings of a midlife paunch that gave him an appealing softness. I enjoyed talking with him and he showed no signs of being put off by my fumbling Spanish. That he judged me to be a worthy partner renewed my confidence and sense of purpose. When it was time to part, I held out my hand again, then hesitated and leaned forward to give him my cheek. In the confusion, I lost my balance and stumbled, bumping him. We managed to shake hands, but I was left feeling as maladroit as a twelve-year-old at a junior high school dance. Once Enrique was gone, I turned to Norberto.

"You should have kissed him goodbye," he admonished, looking uncharacteristically stern. "A hand shake is very formal—pre-revolutionary in fact. Since *el triunfo,* people are much more affectionate with one another."

At our next meeting, Enrique and I became kissing colleagues.

Enrique and his family lived on a quiet tree-lined street of Vedado in a compact first-floor apartment of a three-story cement building. His apartment was tucked behind a gated patio and a driveway into which he could barely squeeze his green Moskavitch, a ramshackle Russian car from the 1980s with which he had a love-hate relationship. His family occupied five small rooms, including a tiny kitchen and a tiny bath. Overloaded bookcases covered every available wall. This was Enrique's childhood home and, due to chronic housing shortages, he had brought his wife Belkis to live there when they married. The couple shared the apartment with their teenage son Enriquito, when he was not away at a state-run boarding school, and Enrique's father. Adding his presence to an already crowded abode was a Great Dane named Emilord who—when not loose in the house—was kept in a miniscule rear patio which also housed Enrique's orchid collection.

Sometimes Enrique and I met at his house to talk. At other times we met in hotel lobbies and restaurants where I always picked up the tab—the only reasonable way to deal with the economic chasm between us. Coffee or *cerveza*, both produced in Cuba, were available only in dollars. His salary was the equivalent of less than forty dollars a month paid entirely in pesos. Mine was exponentially greater. Over time we met more often at his house where Belkis' generous lunches balanced our transactions in the dollar economy.

I usually called ahead, but even when I appeared at his front gate unannounced, Enrique welcomed me as if he knew I was coming, always with a warm *"Hola, Juanita,"* a kiss on the cheek, and a *cafecito.* Enrique liked his with lots of sugar. I asked for mine with *sólo un poquito.* Belkis cheerfully obliged us both. I became increasingly comfortable dropping by for coffee and conversation, and Enrique didn't seem to tire of my questions about his culture, the medical system, the embargo, or the troubled economy of Cuba.

Like his compatriots, Enrique referred to the U.S. embargo as *"el bloqueo,"* using the language of war rather than of trade. As he saw it, the blockade profoundly affected the health of Cubans. Except for drugs manufactured on the island, pharmaceuticals were in short supply and their availability was unpredictable, since Cuba could not purchase them from the States or from any company abroad that was a U.S. subsidiary. Shortages of antibiotics and analgesics were chronic and severe, and often only one type of antibiotic was available—sometimes penicillin, other times tetracycline.

In part as a result of such scarcities, the government had begun to invest in the development of alternative medicine, "green medicine" as it was called. At some clinics, acupuncture, massage, floral therapy, and mud treatments were offered alongside more traditional fare. I remembered a visit to an herbal medicine farm in Nicaragua that I had made shortly after the end of the Contra War and the defeat of the *Sandinista* government. Herbal medicine was being promoted while the health care infrastructure that the *Sandinistas* had established was being dismantled. The Nicaraguans who worked on the farm were proud, bolstered by rhetoric that glorified the wisdom of their ancestors. But the efficacy of herbal treatments had not been scientifically established, and the herbs were a poor substitute for what was no longer available: medicines and a functioning public health safety net. It was unclear to me if the *medicina verde* movement in Cuba was a good or bad omen.

In Enrique's front sitting room, fueled by caffeine, sugar, and budding friendship, we worked on the details of our collaboration, with occasional interruptions when neighbors stopped by to say hello. Together we designed a questionnaire for family doctors about how they dealt with shortages of pharmaceuticals and medical supplies. It was detailed, several pages long, and one which, given enough respondents, would enable us to quantify patterns with statistical rigor. Using the findings from the survey, we would develop a protocol for focus group discussions and in-depth interviews of doctors and patients. This second phase would allow us to supplement our numerical analysis with illustrative case examples. Ours was a methodology that even my scientific father would have approved.

Enrique thought Old Havana would be the perfect site for our work and he was confident that his medical contacts there would help us. I was thrilled at the possibility of working amidst seventeenth century buildings surrounded by remnants of the old city walls.

I was surprised to learn that there were more than enough physicians in Old Havana to carry out a respectable scientific survey. By Enrique's estimates, the population there was served by over five hundred family physicians—hard to believe given that I could cover most of the municipality on foot in an afternoon. Each physician teamed with a nurse and cared for about two hundred and fifty families living in their barrio.

Never could I conduct such a project by myself in Cuba, but I trusted that Enrique would be an energetic collaborator and guide. As we refined our plans, my fantasy life took off. I imagined pouring over questionnaires and entering numbers on spreadsheets. With dictionary at my side, I would decipher handwritten responses in the pursuit of Truth. Physicians would pour out their hearts about how they couldn't care for their patients, ever appreciative of my benevolent listening and eagerness to understand their experience. I pictured myself interviewing gravely ill Cubans on their death beds in the nooks and crannies of apartments and s*oláres* of Old Havana. I imagined them cursing the United States government for their unnecessary suffering and lamenting how their health tragedies could have been avoided. In my mind's eye, my Spanish was fluent, my comprehension complete, and my interpersonal sensitivities boundless. I was the perfect muckraker.

chapter 5

Enrique's hands were deep in the maw of his Moskavitch when I dropped by. He peered at me over his glasses with a look of amused exasperation as he tried to discern why the old car was sputtering this time. "It's a Trashkovitch!" he muttered. He wiped his hands on a rag and followed me into his house.

This being Cuba, he explained, our proposal had to be approved by the *Ministerio de Salud Pública.* He was hopeful that MINSAP, as it was called, would grant us a go-ahead since ours was a collaborative venture and not one generated by a North American alone. Besides, we would document the harmful effects of the embargo, a goal in line with the dominant rhetoric of Cuba. Our optimism was buoyed by Bob Schwartz, the director of DISARM, a humanitarian organization working against the embargo. He had regular contact with MINSAP officials, and, upon hearing of our proposal, offered his support and practical advice.

Application needed to be made through the ministry's office of international relations. As the foreigner in the collaboration, the responsibility for pursuing approval fell to me, while behind the scenes Enrique and Bob coached me on what to do next. I tried to do as I was told, and enjoyed the sense of mission shared across the Cuba/U.S. divide. Gathering data that could be used against *el bloqueo* felt like a worthy endeavor.

The prospect of dealing with health ministers immediately made my Spanish tutors all the more important. Responding to my urgency, Sarán and Henri devised role-plays that included dialogues with hypothetical MINSAP officials. "Never be too direct with governmental superiors," they warned. "Whenever you can, use the deferent form of the subjunctive—'*pudiera*' (might you?) instead of the simple indicative—'*puede*' (will you?)."

MINSAP occupied a decrepit high-rise on La Rampa. My contact there was Dr. Portilla, a wrinkled and tired-looking man who was probably in his prime during the early days of the revolution. Enrique and Bob agreed that I should visit him frequently, first to submit our written proposal and respond to his questions and then to keep the pressure on. They were adamant in urging gentle harassment as the Cuban way, though even dropping by several times a week felt rude to me. Still, backed by their encouragement I overrode my Emily Post upbringing and called on Dr. Portilla often, hoping my "*pudieras*" would soften any negative effects of my persistence.

At the front of the building, I encountered a uniformed guard who sometimes waved me through and other times required me to register at an office in the basement where an official examined my passport and issued me a pass. Which procedure would be followed on a given day remained a mystery. Once cleared I would walk by the black and white Wilfred Lam mosaic that gave 1950s ambience to the lobby and down to the wing of offices dedicated to MINSAP's international affairs.

Furnishings there were spare. The old wooden chairs and brittle plastic upholstery looked as worn as the people who sat in them. First impressions didn't inspire optimism. Nevertheless, Dr. Portilla was perpetually hospitable and ever willing to meet with me on the status of the proposal.

"Yes," he assured, "I received your proposal."

"Yes," he assured, "I received your clarifications of my questions."

"Yes," he assured, "the proposal is being reviewed by the Vice-Minister."

"No, I can't give you a definite answer yet."

"No, I don't know when I will be able to."

"No, I have no more news or suggestions."

At each meeting we engaged in a slight variant of this exchange, always culminating in a kind *despedida.* Dr. Portilla often personally showed me out, walking me to the front door of the building and giving me a kiss on the cheek.

The only toilet paper in the restroom closest to the international office of MINSAP consisted of already printed-on computer paper. With each successive visit, I became more convinced that the restroom was supplied with proposals such as ours. One day Enrique and I were discussing our lack of progress with MINSAP while eating *platos típicos* at an upscale café in Old Havana. Next to my plate where a paper napkin should have been, the waiter had placed a carefully folded length of toilet tissue.

~

In the gaps between frustrating MINSAP visits, Enrique came up with excursions that he thought would fit my professional agenda. One morning he invited me to visit a family doctor who worked in a neighborhood *consultorio* in Central Havana. The waiting room and consulting office were almost bare of furniture and there was little evidence of medical equipment. The young doctor and I spoke privately, sitting at his wooden desk under an AIDS prevention poster. He had just finished a morning of seeing patients.

"What do you like most about your work?" I ventured to ask.

"Sembrando mis pacientes," he responded, without hesitation. Growing my patients. Surprised by his odd response, I asked him to elaborate.

"I find it very gratifying when one of my patients stops smoking or when a woman gets pregnant at just the right time for her family. And I like it when I am able to help a patient avoid complications from an illness."

Our conversation turned to the recent outbreak of dengue fever. There had been two cases among the two hundred and some families he cared for. He was pleased that the community he served had been so well-informed that family members had identified the affected individuals early in the illness. With prompt hospitalization, both had survived.

Was this doctor's emphasis on prevention and education typical, I wondered? Was he for real or parroting the public relations curriculum of a Cuban medical education? How might doctors in the United States talk about their work if, like their Cuban counterparts, they assumed responsibility for the health of a defined population rather than for self-selected individuals? I thought of my medical colleagues at home working long hours in clinics and hospitals. Their incomes were directly related to how many diseases they diagnosed and how many medical procedures they performed and coded on insurance forms. Where were the hours and incentives for them to educate patients to stay well? And how did Cuban doctors have time to treat illness, with so much focus on prevention and education? The questions kept coming. I wanted to see more.

"Eres música, poeta, y loca," Enrique exclaimed. You are musician, poet, and crazy person. He was using the Cuban *dicho* for a "jack of all trades," a comment evoked by my being game for just about anything he suggested.

"Would you like to visit my teacher with me?" he asked, already knowing my response. "He's a famous medical historian. His house is just a few blocks away." He paused, catching my eye. "He lives with a cook, a chauffeur, and a butler—and he's a Marxist!" Enrique grinned with delight at sharing this jewel of contradiction.

We walked briskly through residential neighborhoods of Vedado. I kept my eyes on the ever-changing terrain of broken sidewalks and missing curbs as Enrique told me about his mentor, now ninety years old. His name was José López Sánchez and he was Professor Emeritus of The University of Havana, a recent winner of *El Premio Nacional de Ciencias Sociales*, and a distinguished senior statesman. His achievements, as Enrique described them, were impressive. José López Sánchez had been a soldier, scientist, writer, and diplomat. In the 1930s he had fought against Franco's nationalists in the Spanish Civil War. He was jailed twice under Batista for his political activities. Since the revolution, he had served as ambassador to Switzerland, India, Afghanistan, Bangladesh, and Nepal. He was Cuba's most distinguished historian of medicine and author of the definitive biography of Cuban scientist Carlos Finlay, a national hero who had been nominated for a Nobel Prize for his work on yellow fever.

We crossed a broad street lined with large trees and entered the patio of an attractive and generously sized two-story home. Enrique rang the buzzer and we were greeted by Milagros, a handsome black woman who had been the old man's cook for many years. She escorted us up a dark internal staircase and we emerged into light on the second floor. There we awaited our host.

I looked around. The living room was richly furnished, the walls adorned with large original paintings. Tropical plants, grillwork on the windows, and a large decorative screen graced the room. There was a TV and VCR, items suggesting either access to dollars or relatives in Miami. A hand fan painted with birds sat in a vase on the coffee table.

My reverie was broken by the shushing sound of slippers on floor. I looked up to see a pale old man in a green striped shirt and turquoise pajama pants pushing his walker into the room. He was unshaven and wearing thick yellowed glasses. His face was chalky white and hung long, as if painted by El Greco. He looked like he had been a man of considerable physical stature before age had settled on his shoulders. As if in slow-motion, he maneuvered himself into a chair. "*No es fácil,*" he mumbled, as if we couldn't tell.

Enrique introduced us, mentioning our common interest in health and Cuban medicine. The old man came to life. "Did you know that I am the oldest Communist in Cuba?" he asked. He rose carefully, shuffled over to his desk, and fumbled through papers, producing a dog-eared yellow document. It was a Communist Party membership card dated 1932, almost thirty years older than the Cuban Revolution. I held it in my hand as if it were the Holy Grail, treasuring the moment.

I expressed my amazement. The old man tucked the card back in his desk, shuffled slowly across the room, and settled again into his chair. Milagros arrived with coffee, and our conversation shifted to a discussion of the Cuban health system.

As vice-minister for public health in the sixties, Dr. López Sánchez had helped develop the socialized medical system, but his feelings were mixed about its subsequent success. On the positive side, he lauded the integration of public health and therapeutic medicine under one state ministry. However, he was disturbed by the poor condition of hospital buildings. There were only two that he thought were still in good shape: the Hospital Nacional Hermanos Ameijeiras, a facility on the Malecón in Central Havana known for providing care to patients who flew in from all over Latin

America, and a second hospital which served the leaders of government and was as spiffy as an upscale hotel.

The doctor faulted *el bloqueo* for many problems. Only with the help of friends or family in other countries could one gain access to needed drugs. Up-to-date medical books published abroad were scarce. Medical students were using texts from the eighties and virtually no medical journals had been regularly available since the early nineties.

Our host changed the subject.

"What do you think about the war in Afghanistan?" he asked, referring to the bellicose response of the United States after 9/11. Before I could respond, he volunteered his own opinions, resting his arms on his walker as he spoke.

"Thirty years ago, when I was ambassador to Afghanistan, the United States had a compelling interest in the region—for its mineral resources and its strategic location. It is obvious that the United States is attacking Afghanistan because of economic and political reasons. Terrorism is pretext," he asserted. "To understand the roots of terrorism, the United States should look within its own borders." I felt momentarily cowed, as if he had mandated personal self-examination.

The old man looked fatigued. Milagros took our empty coffee cups. It was time to go. But before we parted, he located a copy of his biography of Carlos Finlay, carefully inscribing the large green volume— *"Para Juanita, por tu visita tan cortés,"* for your very gracious visit. As I took a moment to read the inscription, his energy rallied and he directed a final question my way. Did I know that Carlos Finlay, not Walter Reed, was responsible for the eradication of yellow fever? Finlay, he said, was the first to identify the *Aedes aegypti* mosquito as the disease vector, although credit for his work had been usurped by the North American.

We exchanged goodbyes. He invited me to visit his personal library on the first floor before we left, a resource he could no longer directly enjoy since he couldn't manage the stairs. Enrique and I descended the stairs and entered the library, room after room filled floor to ceiling with bookcases. Over four thousand volumes were carefully arranged on shelves, organized by such topics as the history of medicine, world literature, Russian encyclopedias, and Cuban writers. Enrique was familiar with every shelf. "This," he said, opening his arms wide, "is the best and most complete library on the history of medicine and science in Cuba."

One glance took in the *Encyclopedia Britannica, The Grand Soviet Encyclopedia,* and the complete twenty-eight-volume set of the works of José Martí. On another shelf was the original dissertation of Tomas Romay Cachón, published in 1797 and entitled *The Malignant Fever commonly called Black Vomit*—an account of a yellow fever epidemic in the West Indies.

As a fellow bibliophile, I feasted on the abundance of rare and valuable bound books, but the air was musty and humid, and many tomes were in sore need of repair. I contemplated the evidence of time passing on the oil-hungry bindings and thought of a bookbinder friend in Ohio who would gladly dedicate his talents to this collection. The oldest of Communists had done admirably well for himself, I thought, but keeping the treasures he had acquired in good condition was beyond what the state he supported could provide.

Milagros, his cook, showed us out.

chapter 6

The broad avenue of the Malecón runs along the shoreline for eight kilometers between Old Havana and the Almendares River that marks the western edge of Vedado. As a newcomer I could always regain my bearings by heading toward the Malecón. I quickly learned to avoid doing so at midday when the asphalt baked all on its surface. Pedestrian traffic was sparse there before dusk, except for occasional fishermen and young boys who played on the rocks beyond the sea wall, but as the temperature dropped in the late afternoon and early evening, people poured onto the boulevard. First, families with children came and young men eager to cast lines and bring home red snapper for dinner, and later, young lovers who snuggled on the wall under the starry sky as men with guitars offered songs for tips.

One day as I hiked toward the Malecón from Old Havana, my eye was caught by the juxtaposition of glowing colors in the soft light—mint green wall, red car, yellow wall, bright blue building. I stopped, mesmerized by the vibration of hues and surfaces.

This was a city for painters, I thought. I had loved painting water-colors when I was young, my soul fed by the meditation of brush on paper and colors diffusing into each other. Had I not chosen psychology, I might have become an artist, but I hadn't touched pigments in years. The ache of lost possibility niggled to the surface. I jerked myself back to the present. At least I could take a picture, maybe even use it to inspire me to find my old paints. I pulled my camera out of my knapsack. As I focused, a young man popped into the frame, smiling and waving, his long black arms and white shirt contrasting with the vivid colors. I snapped the shutter.

He approached and gestured that he wanted to write down his address for me so I could send him the photo. Having no faith in the United States/Cuba mail and not wanting to make a promise I could not keep, I said that, regretfully, this would not be possible. He shrugged, nonchalant, and beckoned to a girl walking by with a tray of candies. Taking one, he handed her a coin and offered the candy to me, his kindness as sweet as what I held in my hand. He ambled off. I bit into the hard, sugary knob. With the first chew, I felt something give and realized that a large filling was now attached to the candy. My tongue poked the ditch left behind.

Damn. I would need a dentist. Much as I'd been enjoying stumbling into the unexpected, this wasn't what I had in mind. I mulled over my options. In my Peace Corps days, I had acquired a dread of dentistry from three hours in the chair of a Nicaraguan butcher who removed four impacted wisdom teeth while short on anesthetics and bedside manner. Ever since, I had fought a propensity to tremble during even minor procedures. Many a dentist had seen me sweat. How would a Cuban dentist treat a borderline dental phobic? Would they have adequate pain-killers—or put me out?

These were my choices: I could go to a regular dental clinic for Cubans or I could go to a state dental clinic specifically for foreign visitors. I had read that the tourist clinics were state-of-the-art and, while expensive by Cuban standards, a bargain compared to health care in the United States. This appealed as the safer option, dental adventure not being my forte. Still, if I could get attention at a neighborhood clinic, I would learn firsthand about the care ordinary Cubans received, and it would be cheaper, maybe even free.

Sharing my dilemma with Dulce and Norberto evoked their most magnanimous caretaking. As they saw it, there was only one choice, since being seen at the tourist clinic would be astronomically expensive in comparison to the nominal cost of seeing their dentist at the neighborhood clinic. But there was a catch. The clinic wouldn't provide me with care if they knew I wasn't one of them. I needed to be a relative, visiting from abroad.

"No pr—ooo—blem," Norberto crooned with a grin. "You are married to my cousin in Miami and visiting your family in Cuba!" He slapped his side and whooped in delight at this prospect. Rummaging through the drawer of the bureau next to the television, he pulled out a videotape and waved it in his hand. *"¿Quieres conocer a tu esposo?"* he asked. "Would you like to meet your husband?"

He slid the cassette into the VCR and I was transported to Hialeah, Florida and an apartment filled with plump Cubans, their girths suggesting familiarity with fast food. There he was, my "husband," bald and beer-bellied, standing with his wife and daughter, showing off his apartment. He waved to us, unaware of his impending bigamy.

Dulce called the dentist and made an appointment for the following Tuesday. The dentist couldn't see me earlier because the compressor for her drill was broken, but it would be fixed by the time I was to see her. Norberto assured me that she had excellent equipment and plenty of medicine since her family in Miami regularly sent her supplies to supplement what the state provided. She was compassionate too, he added, and skillful at managing pain. Two years earlier, when he had fallen off his bicycle and landed on his face, she had extracted his two loosened front teeth and replaced them with prosthetic ones. "It barely hurt," he pronounced, then opened his mouth and pointed to his prominent front teeth. I resolved not to ride a bike through the streets of Havana.

On the following Monday evening at supper, Dulce told me that the compressor was still broken and my dental appointment was on hold pending its repair. She was apologetic; I was relieved, ready to be spared the experience. Later, as I prepared for bed, Dulce knocked on the door to my room. "Look," she said, "The compressor could get fixed at any time, and you need to be ready." She held up a freshly ironed housedress on a hanger. "It will be perfect for the occasion," she said, obviously pleased with her forethought. I looked at the flimsy gray and white shift and was thinking that these were definitely not my colors when she interrupted my thoughts.

"¿Y los zapatos?" she queried, looking down at the sturdy tie shoes I had just removed. They still looked new and the thick soles were just beginning to show wear.

"No Cuban wears shoes like those," she insisted, but not to worry. She had thought of that too, and when the day came for my appointment, she would lend me her sandals.

I hung the dress on the rod that passed for a closet in my room. There it stayed for the rest of the month, alternately evoking my amusement at the thought of wearing it and relief that the compressor was never fixed. In the end, I had a sample of the Cuban experience of health care; elusive replacement parts resulting in delay, in a theoretically excellent system. "Research on health care," I mused, as my tongue circled the cavern in my tooth. My dentist in Ohio would be happy to see me.

Two expressions were ever in the air, spouted in public places and repeated by Enrique and Dulce and Norberto in every conceivable context: *"¡Es Cuba!"* It's Cuba, the all-purpose explanation often accompanied by a shrug of the shoulders, and *"¡No es fácil!"* It's not easy. I was beginning to appreciate both. My first month would soon be over, and Enrique and I still had no definitive word from MINSAP. It was becoming apparent that their review and approval would take more time and that I was destined to resume visits to Dr. Portilla when I returned in January. But my spirits were high. Bob and Enrique remained optimistic that our project would eventually be approved, and I was confident that they knew more than I did.

Besides, awaiting a response from MINSAP, I was enjoying lively and informative explorations, thanks to Enrique. Maybe if we didn't get the official go-ahead, I would redefine what I considered acceptable "research on health care" or maybe discard the rules altogether. Wasn't I conducting research whenever and however I asked people about any aspect of health? And wasn't "health" a topic that could encompass most of life?

chapter 7

Challenges zoomed toward me faster than I could lob them back over the cross-cultural net. The constant struggle to project a semblance of coping and competence was exhausting. I was wearing out. One afternoon after trudging across Central Havana, I collapsed with fatigue at the outdoor café of Hotel Inglaterra from where I could look across the park to the edge of Old Havana. My legs tingled. My blouse was moist with sweat. I thought of other solo travelers who may have rested at this same spot. This café had been the favorite haunt of journalists during the Spanish-American War and I wondered how many of them had traveled alone and what thoughts they had harbored sitting at these tables.

Sipping lemonade and feeling lonely, I watched the street life in front of me. A band of teenagers in navy and white uniforms tooted an afternoon concert to those passing by. A crowd gathered to listen. Nearby three old men played dominoes under the trees, their conversation punctuated with the smack of black tiles. There was so much life in this in-between, in this space that separated the old from the very old sections of the city.

So much happens in between. And that's where I felt too, neither completely in one country or the other, in between the exhilarating fright of being alone and the solace of company, in between my needing to know what my next steps would be and accepting what was: the Brownian motion of chance and possibility.

The shore of my familiar self felt distant and I was treading water, too far out to turn around but with no new shoreline yet in view. I was bobbing along in strong currents, trying to negotiate the open seas in my makeshift raft of boards and rubber tires.

I looked over at the next table where a lanky blond man sat alone. He was about my age and handsome, but with the weary look of one who had traveled too many miles without a change of socks. He gestured to the waiter for coffee and opened a book in his lap. His face disappeared behind a shag of yellow-silver hair as he leaned into his reading, and I wondered if he were Scandinavian, perhaps a distant relative of mine. Should I reach out to this fellow traveler and attempt to bridge between our solitary selves?

I imagined starting a conversation with him, knowing that, though neither young nor beautiful, I could seduce him that far. For a spell I allowed myself the comfort of fantasy and pondered what it would be like to have a love affair with a Nordic stranger in Havana. He glanced up and our eyes met. I wavered and we both looked away. No, I thought, checking the impulse to salve angst with conversation. Better to stay quiet and befriend this in-between, strangely fertile with possibility.

Later when I finished my lemonade, I left my spot of contemplation to stroll past the landmark bronze lions at the head of Paseo del Prado, the magnificent tree-lined boulevard that traced the seam between Old Havana and Central Havana. Through the sycamore trees I could appreciate the views on either side.

~

Being in Cuba alone was far more taxing than I had anticipated it would be. Bound by cobwebs of linguistic frustration, I yearned for deeper communication with people around me than my Spanish could sustain. Adaptation required constant expenditure of energy. I was finding it difficult to pay attention or remember, as if my brain were developing a slick protective coating to prevent further stress. My mind careened away from anything new. Visions of home intruded and lingered. I imagined opening my refrigerator in Ohio and finding broccoli or my favorite coffee ice cream. I missed the *being known* that went with being in my own culture. I missed feeling like an adult most of the time. I longed to share a glass of wine with Phil at the end of the day without expectation of talk.

My thoughts drifted back more than thirty years to the summer after my junior year in college. I had held a summer job working with mentally handicapped children, commuting to a day camp from the security of my parental home. The same summer, Phil traded all the quarters he had saved in a huge glass jar for a plane ticket to Luxemburg. There he purchased a motor scooter, and for several months, explored the back roads of Europe and ventured into Russia by himself. The hedgehogs that sought the warmth of his sleeping bag were his only company. It never occurred to me then to envy his solo journey nor to pursue one of my own. Instead I waited eagerly for his letters, needing to hear that he missed me. I'd been lost in the miasma of 1960s femininity, caught in passive voice.

Finally it dawned on me that I was making up now for what I couldn't imagine for myself then. I was claiming the right to be in the world *all by myself* without a partner or a parent. I was claiming the right to say yes to adventures of my own choosing and to feel the contours of my aloneness without Mom and Dad or Phil to watch over me or protect me from harm. In my fifties I was struggling with conflicts of late adolescence. As these realizations took hold, I found it easier to tolerate feeling linguistically and emotionally spent: these were growing pains.

In the days that followed, this fresh awareness added a new layer of meaning to my situation, but I continued to feel escalating fatigue. Thank goodness for the temporary oblivion of sleep, although even that had become problematic. The noise that penetrated the deep recesses of Vedado barely abated in the wee hours of the morning. Each night I sought silence by sticking rubber plugs in my ears, but when I awoke and removed them I was bombarded again. Cars beeped and backfired as men gunned their old engines for one more go. Parrots squawked, sirens whirred, and radios blared. People called to each other at decibel levels that would be rude were it not required to be heard above the racket. An auditory fatigue set in, unlike anything I had ever experienced, and I began to lust for silence with a visceral craving.

I wanted to be completely alone in a very quiet place. *Solita.*

So much for the virtues of cultural immersion—I'd absorbed as large a dose as my system could handle with still a week to go before my departure. Like a New Yorker heading for respite in the woods of Vermont, I decided to leave the city for a few days. My guidebook offered plenty of suggestions for excursions within reach of Havana but distant enough to offer at least relative quiet. I chose a beach about an hour away and mentioned to Dulce and Norberto that I would be going to Playas del Este for a quiet weekend alone.

"I'll be back on Sunday evening."

On Friday morning when I rose for breakfast, my bag packed, I was surprised to find Dulce in street clothes instead of her usual housedress. "I'm going with you," she announced in echo of Day One. She looked pleased.

I gulped my *cafecito.*

Dulce had worked out our itinerary. She had called her son Vladimir, a child of the heyday of Russian influence, who lived near the beach in Guanabo. He had found a rental room for me just down the street from his house. Dulce would accompany me to where Vladimir lived and visit with him for the afternoon. When she returned home that evening, he would show me where to eat, and on Sunday, take me to the bus for my return. She had it all planned.

"That way, I won't worry about you," she said, smiling broadly and patting my arm. "My daughter is going with us too!"

In the face of her delight, I was rendered speechless.

~

It was quiet on the beach of Guanabo, except for the splash and lull of waves and children's voices carried by the soft zephyr of late afternoon. Dulce and her daughter had returned to Havana and thankfully Vladimir didn't share his mother's compulsion to hover. I was alone. I climbed to the top of a vacant lifeguard tower that offered a ninety degree view of the sea. Ten feet above the sand and soothed by the whoosh of palm trees in the balmy air, I spoke to no one, preferring to stare out at the sea and find quiet inside myself. Time passed. I opened a paperback that I had purchased in the Plaza de Armas and sampled the words of a beloved Cuban poet who had lived in Vedado, Dulce María Loynaz.

> The eyes look upon the blue stars; the feet, humbly hugging the earth, support the pedestal for the eyes that look upon the blue stars.

I turned to another page and kept reading.

> There is something very subtle and profound in turning to look back at the traveled road...
> The road where, without leaving a trace, all life has been left.

From my perch looking out to the sea, I considered the "traveled road" behind me. That first day in the Hotel Plaza seemed long ago, not just four weeks. Cuba the abstraction had been replaced by very particular Cubans—Norberto, Dulce, and Enrique. My initial apprehensions and self-doubt had been assuaged by the beginnings of friendship. Paradoxically, the more connected I felt, the more comfortable I was becoming with the idea of leaving the security of Norberto and Dulce's care.

The sun was disappearing behind the palms. Fifty meters down the beach stood a *policía,* his legs apart, hands clasped behind him, scanning the sea horizon. He looked overdressed in his blue and gray uniform, beret, and billy club as two little boys in swim trunks somersaulted in front of him. What was he looking for, his gaze fixed on the Florida Straits, signs of invasion from the north—a repeat of the Bay of Pigs?—or *balseros* leaving the island by sea?

My thoughts turned to my own departure from Cuba. It wouldn't be long until the month was over. Before I left for home and the Christmas holidays, I needed to figure out my living arrangements for January. I didn't feel like Little Juanita anymore. I was ready for more independence, maybe even a place of my own that would allow me to follow my own rhythms of immersion and retreat. In my whole life, I had never lived completely by myself. It was time.

I thought about the neighborhoods that I had seen on my urban meanderings, and trying them out in my mind, I gave rein to possibilities. It would be good to be closer to where Enrique and I intended to work. Maybe I could find an apartment in Old Havana. Dulce and Norberto could visit.

chapter 8

With cobbled streets opening onto sunny plazas, and doorways offering enticing glimpses of the life within, Old Havana held seductive allure beyond what I wanted to resist. I'd never lived in the midst of still-breathing ruins. I'd never even lived in a dense urban environment. I wanted to do both.

Enrique's brow furrowed when I told him my plan. I tried to be persuasive. If MINSAP approved our proposal we would be conducting our study there, and living in the same community where I worked would be wonderfully convenient. Gathering impressions informally would complement our more formal research approach. I pictured myself mingling with neighbors and listening to their stories about sick children and problems finding medicine. But Enrique was adamant in his opposition. It was one thing to work there, he warned, but another to live there by myself. The streets were dark and dimly lit and it wouldn't be safe for me to come and go after sunset. Why didn't I stay in Vedado instead and move closer to where he lived?

I bristled at his protectiveness. He was beginning to feel like an overly watchful older brother, and I wasn't of a mind to bow to any male authority. I thought he underestimated my ability to get along independently; after all, he hadn't met my intrepid mother. I wouldn't be deterred.

There were no classified ads in *Granma* and from my experience with Norberto and Dulce, I knew that most housing options, especially the cheaper ones, were clandestine as they lacked the required state license. Gone was any fear of renting a room not officially sanctioned. I figured that the landlord, not I, would bear the risk.

I had heard that the best way to find options was by word of mouth on the street, so one morning I set off for Central Park and the spot where men gathered to talk baseball. A more experienced foreign visitor had suggested that I seek help from a baseball aficionado known as "the office manager" and identifiable by his Rastafarian braids and multi-colored crocheted hat. I spotted him immediately and waved to get his attention. He separated from the pack and introduced himself as Tito. Of course, he said, he'd be happy to show me some rentals.

The two of us dodged taxis, bicycles, and foot traffic to cut into Old Havana by the Bacardi building, an art deco masterpiece from the thirties in the process of restoration. Details in ochre, rust, and white terra cotta blazed bright against the blue sky. We passed under a banner that stretched across the street declaring, "*En cada barrio, revolución*" (In every neighborhood, revolution), and then entered the narrow cacophonous streets with their gritty beauty of colonial decay.

Tito fielded greetings on every block. Upon turning down Calle Compostela we were forced to make a quick detour as an opaque grey-brown cloud expanded rapidly into the street ahead of us. Fire, I thought, ready to run. "Dengue," my guide offered, reading my thoughts. Before diverting down a side street, I could see exterminators from the health ministry spraying for the mosquitoes that carried the deadly disease.

Over several hours we crisscrossed neighborhoods, in and out of buildings that appeared uninhabitable from the outside but livable if unappealing behind the portals. One apartment was accessible only by a poorly lit and steamy elevator that—to my eye—would accommodate one person. Tito and I managed to squeeze in. To my amazement, a mole of a woman was sitting on a stool tucked into the blackest corner of the lift, her job to push the buttons of the tiny tin-can transport all day long. Good God, I thought. Not only did she have an office without windows, she had neither air nor light and probably earned less than ten dollars a month. We were an odd threesome, and the humidity in the compressed space and the ponderous climb made me woozy. I flashed on Sartre's *No Exit* with its plot of eternal confinement amid strangers, and willed my claustrophobia to pass.

The ride to the fifth floor took forever, but we finally came to a stop with a bump and a squeak, and the door opened to an apartment flooded with sunlight and offering a fabulous view of the city. Unfortunately, only one small room was available within quarters already crowded with a new baby. I decided to pass.

That rental was typical. Rooms rented for about twenty dollars a day with tight quarters and minimal privacy. Bathrooms were shared with families pressed by the need to rent space to earn hard currency. None was legal. None offered the space and independence I sought.

At every stop someone suggested yet another prospect for housing, and each visit ended with a flurried exchange as Tito elicited specifics. Only later did I realize that this system was lubricated with cash, each referral source positioning for a finder's fee contingent on where I finally chose to live.

When we returned to the streets, a black woman in skin-tight scarlet pants rushed toward Tito. She jabbered loudly, her breasts bobbing in her tank top, waving her arms in invitation. She had a room she wanted to show me. Her name was Nancy and we followed her beyond the façade of an ancient building through obscure passageways and up a circular stone staircase, one story, then two, then three. Sweat was running down the back of my neck. There were no hand rails and the steps were very narrow and deeply worn. Climbing through the tight vertical space surrounded by crumbling walls, I couldn't imagine retracing my steps with luggage. By the time we reached the floor where Nancy lived, I was laboring from exertion and heat.

She opened a door to a grim apartment almost empty of furniture except for the single room available for rent. There next to a dresser a pink flowered spread neatly covered a double bed. The room could be mine for just ten dollars a day and she would do laundry for me besides. No bargain—I would risk a fatal fall with each coming or going.

I complimented Nancy on the room but begged off. Briefly she looked crest-fallen, but then reanimated. "I know another place that would be perfect for you—just down the street—a whole apartment just for you. *Ven conmigo.*" In no time I was weaving through the crowded streets again, now with Tito and Nancy at either side. Locals, mostly men, all shades of brown, eyed me curiously from open doorways.

We walked several blocks to the end of Calle San Juan de Dios. In front of a heap of rubble in the middle of the street, we turned into the entrance of a boxy apartment complex that might have been new when Castro came to power. A flight of stairs led us to a landing where a small bra factory was visible through shuttered windows. We ascended to a second landing, rimmed with potted philodendrons and ferns. Several apartments opened onto this patio. The building was shabby, but the architecture and décor were of the sixties, perfect for a lodger of my generation. The apartment for rent was even legal. I felt hopeful.

The landlord, a man named Ariel, unbolted two sets of locks to open the door and welcome us. He was about forty, a meek ectomorph of Spanish descent with a pallor that suggested that he rarely saw the sun. He introduced me to his wife, Rosita, who resembled him to a remarkable degree.

I surveyed the spacious room we had entered. It was airy and bright, with yellow walls and simple wooden furniture. A tape player with a stack of music cassettes sat on a shelf between plastic speakers. A Mona Lisa and a Madonna and Child hung side by side on one wall and faced a pair of Playboy centerfold look-alikes on the other. Was Ariel the decorator? I wondered: were these female images stand-ins for his instinctual conflicts? There was nothing in his physical presence that suggested passion of any kind; his black hairline was receding, his eyes were dark lidded slits behind glass, his shirt was pale and indistinct. He sported a dark Charlie Chaplin mustache but lacked a sense of humor.

A galley kitchen took up most of the far wall. Above cupboards and supported by boards were five fifty-gallon containers which I would soon discover roared like a waterfall for an hour each morning as they filled with water. A door at the end of the kitchen led to a bedroom where a mirrored mahogany dresser dwarfed a double bed. The sheets looked like cellophane and the pillow case crackled when I touched it. Tall slatted windows overlooked putty-colored roof tops that hop-scotched to the horizon and the sea. I loved the very foreignness of the view.

I paused and felt a flush of pride in what I had accomplished. On my own steam I had found my way out of my windowless office and into this fascinating country, this unique adventure, this tour with Tito, and this peculiar moment. And now because of choices already made, I could choose to live in this apartment and claim the view from these windows as my own.

Only the bathroom was a bit of a disappointment. There was a simple shower, sink, and an old cracked toilet empty of water and without a seat. Ariel, following close behind me, assured that the seat would appear by the time I returned and that flushing was easy with a pail of water. He would show me.

I wanted to lunge at the chance to rent Ariel's apartment, but I held back, hearing Enrique's cautions in my head. I hesitated, unsure of whether I wanted to concede to his wishes or act on my own, aware that this conflict between external authority and self-determination was becoming a theme of my Havana life. Caution won. I told Ariel that I wanted to think it over and get back with him in a few days. I thanked Tito and tipped him three dollars for his half day's work. I offered to tip Nancy too but she declined. *"La amistad tiene más valor que el dinero,"* she said, as if I were a dear friend. Friendship has more value than money. Then she added, "Maybe tomorrow when my child is sick, you can help me with medicine." I should have been suspicious.

The following afternoon I felt compelled to return to the apartment for a second look. I was sure that I could find it by myself but instead found myself wandering, unable to locate the heap of rubble that identified the right street and building. I hated to admit that I needed directions, but finally I did and tagged a friendly pubescent lad who had been watching me. I pulled on my bra strap and asked him to take me to *la fabrica.* His face lit with recognition and within a turn or two, he left me exactly where I needed to be and ran off gleefully with a dollar *propino.*

Ariel and Rosita were happy to see me. Rosita fixed tea and the three of us sat in the *sala.* I knew that even my adventurous mother might have worries similar to Enrique's, so I asked Ariel about the safety of the neighborhood, the lights in the stairwell, the neighbors, and the locks. *"No se preocupe,"* he reassured. They lived just a block away and would help me with anything I needed.

"Do you know that you can dry your laundry on the roof of the building?" he asked. He showed an uncanny knowledge of what would tempt me further. "And perhaps there are adjustments that I could make so the apartment would be more appealing to you? I can remove the religious pictures, if you want, or take down the pictures of the naked women if they offend you."

He repeated the price—just twenty dollars a day. He would include breakfast each morning and show me where to shop for other meals.

Ariel saw me glance at his computer in the corner. "Do you like poetry?" he inquired in bizarre non-sequitur. *"Claro que sí,"* I replied, my interest piqued. I loved the work of Chilean poet Pablo Neruda, I told him, and had just discovered Dulce María Loynaz. "Do you like poetry too?" I asked hopefully. He answered by pivoting in his chair until he faced the computer. He adjusted his glasses and punched a finger to the keyboard. With a click the black screen faded and a bare-breasted woman posed demurely on his screensaver. He clicked again and she faded into oblivion as stanza after stanza of poetry took her place.

It was José Martí who finally seduced me into renting Ariel's apartment, for on the screen was a poem beloved by Cuban school-children and adults alike, *Los Zapaticos de Rosa.* Ariel recited line after line with great feeling that belied his meek demeanor. Merging with the words, he animated and I sensed a passion for language bubbling just below the surface. My rental hesitations dissolved with thoughts of afternoon salons with tea, José Martí, and the tutelage of my poet landlord.

"Yes," I said. "I want the apartment for the month of January at least."

I was settled in my decision and Enrique accepted his defeat graciously. But it wasn't to be quite so easy. Several days later, Ariel phoned me at Norberto and Dulce's. There was a problem that we needed to discuss face to face. I agreed to stop by to talk with him the following afternoon. I mentioned to Dulce my surprise that Ariel wouldn't share his concern on the telephone. "Remember where you are, Juanita!" she said. "Many people here are afraid to talk on the phone because sometimes you hear another line cut in. If there is any illegal aspect to what you are doing, this can be a problem."

When I arrived at the apartment, Ariel looked distressed. Much as he wanted to rent the apartment to me for twenty dollars a day, he could not. Nancy had approached him, he said, demanding a finder's fee of five dollars a day and threatening physical attack if he didn't pay up. He punched the air with his fists to make sure I understood. She had the right to her fee, he added. This was the way things were done. If I couldn't pay twenty-five dollars a day, he would help me find another apartment. *"La amistad tiene más valor que el dinero,"* he said. This time, the expression struck me as disingenuous, arousing suspicion that he and Nancy were in cahoots.

I did the math. If Ariel could collect a finder's fee for helping me locate an alternative place and then rent his apartment to another boarder, he would avoid having to pay Nancy and come out ahead. I was beginning to get the picture: an infinite and intricate web of inter-connected Cubans all vying for the most advantageous position for harvesting dollars.

Twenty-five dollars was more than I wanted to spend, so for the next two hours, I traipsed around Old Havana again, this time with Ariel instead of Tito as my guide. As before, all options involved too tight quarters with too little privacy, and as the sun got hotter and I fatigued, Ariel's rental started looking better even at the higher price. Finally I suggested that we rest at a café, and over *dos cervezas Crystal* I agreed to his terms. He looked relieved then said, "Please, don't mention to Nancy that I showed you other places to live. I don't want trouble with anyone."

For better or worse my search for new lodging was over. I would return in January with the hope of studying José Martí with my poet landlord and hanging my wash out to dry on the roof—just like any other *Habanera.*

part 2

on the ground

chapter 9

For the month of December, I relished the reconnection with family and friends and threw myself into the imperatives of the Christmas holidays. Karin, home from college, matched my rush of Cuba talk with stories of new friends and the challenges of organic chemistry. Phil gladly relinquished kitchen duties in favor of my cooking, and when I discovered all-but-empty ice cream cartons in the freezer, confessed to regular indulgence in my absence. Several times I drove into the village to share coffee and repartee with Jim and Leon and Claude, but I never stopped at my office on the way, afraid that doing so would suck me back into the emotional stew I associated with the space.

In early January, Karin headed back to school and Phil resumed teaching. I flew back to Cuba, ready and eager to exchange the bitter cold of Ohio for Havana sunshine, my mind crowded with images of Havana streets and the faces of friends and acquaintances from my November sojourn. This time my anxiety was born of excitement more than fear of the unknown, although I still felt a touch of apprehension when I thought of our research proposal hanging in the limbo of the health ministry or contemplated living by myself in the yellow apartment above the bra factory.

Still I was optimistic that MINSAP would ultimately approve our project. Bob Schwartz of DISARM, the humanitarian organization working against the embargo, was continuing to cheer me on and had even offered me respite from worries about the Office of Foreign Assets Control (OFAC) by covering my January stay with the specific license of his organization. I thought that a few more visits with Dr. Portilla would likely result in the official go-ahead we needed to begin our research. If we were lucky, Enrique and I would soon be rolling. By day we would interview physicians and patients in neighborhood *consultorios.* By night I would write up notes or listen to music in my apartment, perhaps interrupted by Ariel dropping by with a book of poetry. In my imagination it was all worked out; fragments of earlier experiences mixed with unmet longings to form a strange amalgam. In fact, I had no idea what would happen, either with the proposal or my new living arrangement.

Ariel and I made final arrangements by email. I would stay at a hotel the first night of my return, and the following afternoon he would help me move into the apartment. He had made one last minute request: could I bring him a copy of *Vanidades,* the New Year's issue that contained the latest horoscopes? Locating the magazine at a newsstand in the Cancun Airport was my final task before heading to the Mexicana gate to await my flight to Havana.

When I arrived at the gate area, the rows of chairs for waiting passengers were almost empty. I sat down across from a diminutive old man who was sitting alone, a wooden cane leaning against the seat beside him. He was precariously balanced, tilting far forward from the very edge of his perch, his elbows on his knees, holding an open newspaper in which he was engrossed. Soft wispy white hair and beard framed a rosy wrinkled face into which his features had long ago retreated.

I tried not to stare but felt compelled to sneak peeks as we waited to board our flight. I couldn't imagine what he was doing traveling by himself anywhere, let alone to Cuba. Did he have any idea what he was getting into? How would he cope with the physical challenges of Havana—the heat, the broken sidewalks, the omnipresent street hazards? Suddenly, I felt like a seasoned veteran of Cuba travel.

Our flight was announced and a diverse dozen people moved toward the gate, no two appearing to fit together. Except for me, all were men. I nodded and smiled at the old man as he inched forward, pushing a small brown suitcase on wheels ahead of him. Except for his white hair and pink face, he was a vision in soft browns. His outfit, which would become familiar to me in the days that followed, consisted of brown slacks, a brown wool sweater that buttoned at the collar, thick marled socks, and brown Birkenstocks that suggested that he might be a retired academic—unless perhaps someone who cared about him had recommended such footwear for stability. He moved so tentatively and looked so frail that it crossed my mind that he might die on our short flight.

We boarded the plane and the old man settled into the seat ahead of me. The cabin was half-empty and we each sat alone. I looked around at my male companions and a wave of loneliness passed through me. I thought about my mother who always initiated conversations with strangers and knew I would feel better if I did the same. While I was considering how to make the first move, the old man rescued me, twisting around in his seat to meet my eyes. "What is taking you to Cuba?" he asked. He sounded genuinely interested. His voice was soft and scratchy, with an accent that I couldn't identify. I must have looked as out of place to him as he did to me.

"I'm a university professor on sabbatical," I replied. "I'm going to Cuba to do research and write about health care." It was my usual explanation and one I still believed at the time. He nodded. For the moment my answer sufficed. I shifted the questions to him. His name was Gary MacEoin. He was Irish but had lived most of his life in the States. A journalist, he was traveling on assignment for the *National Catholic Reporter* to write about the state of religion in Cuba. This would be his eleventh working trip to the island since his first in 1945. He would be a guest at the Martin Luther King Center in Maríanao, one of the western municipalities of Havana. The staff there was arranging for him to interview religious and civic leaders during a week-long stay.

I was stunned; he was ninety-two and still pursuing his life work, undeterred by his obvious frailty or the calamitous risks of traveling by himself. My sense of being a seasoned traveler dissolved in the solvent of Gary's experience, and envy crystallized in its stead. Gary had a clear job to accomplish and an organizational host to help him, whereas I was making up each day as I went along. How quickly I flipped from savoring my unfettered circumstances to coveting someone else's defined mission.

"Mind if I join you?" I asked, unbuckling my seatbelt. "Of course not," he replied and I moved to take the empty seat beside him. Close up, he looked no younger. His wrinkled face was elongated by his receded hairline and the droop of age, his delicate skin almost transparent, splotchy from decades in tropical climes. The half-moon creases under his rheumy eyes mirrored the curves of his bushy, untrimmed eyebrows.

Gary's subdued friendliness quickly cut through my incipient loneliness, and we talked for the remainder of the forty-five minute flight. His manner was quiet and gentle, although in the days we would subsequently spend together, I would discover that his countenance could cloud in an instant, lending him a judgmental air. With something I said—wrong apparently — his demeanor would shift, and he would firmly correct my grammar or pronunciation in whichever language my transgression had occurred. At such moments, he reminded me of the stern God-the-Father that I had imagined as a child, and I felt I had disappointed him by failing to rise to his intellectual standards. It was my father all over again, and I found it exasperating that—in my fifties and with the credentials of a mental health professional—I still had to fight the impulse to respond to older men as surrogate dads. If I could just keep God and my father out of the equation, I knew that Gary could teach me a great deal about Cuba and life.

We were to arrive in Havana in the early evening, but with the inevitable delay at customs, I knew we wouldn't be leaving the airport until late. I felt protective of my new acquaintance and decided that the least I could do, being younger and healthier, was to ensure that he arrived safely at his destination. He didn't have an address for the guesthouse where he would be staying, only a phone number, so as the plane descended, I suggested that he accompany me to the hotel in Old Havana where I had a reservation and take a room for the night. In the morning, he could call his contact and make his way to his lodging. He agreed.

Standing in the customs line waiting for clearance, I juggled my laptop and luggage and awkwardly maneuvered Gary's push carry-on. Someone else found him a wheel chair, a concession he was willing to make to bum knees and artificial hips.

It was eleven o'clock when we arrived at the front desk of the Hostel San Isabel where I had a reservation. Gary turned and looked up at me. I felt myself warm to this ancient soul. "If you want," he suggested, in a voice muffled with fatigue, "we could share a room." He paused, sensing my unease. "Over the years I have often shared rooms with women traveling," he said.

I hesitated. He chuckled, "It wouldn't be too exciting for you!"

His invitation was too quick. "Thank you, but I don't think so," I replied, sounding aloof. The words were the same ones I had used years earlier when a fellow I had just met at a college mixer suggested that we go to his car to make out.

Gary paused. "I understand. Then perhaps you would like to join me for a nightcap. I have a bottle of Scotch in my bag."

"Thank you, but I don't think so," I demurred, trying to be firm but friendly, following some internal protocol for limit-setting that my parents would have sanctioned. "I'm awfully tired. How about we meet for breakfast around eight?"

Even as I spoke, I wished that I weren't so beholden to the mandates of caution. I didn't really want to part from his company. And what was the danger? Did I actually think there was risk of sexual assault? No one would even know if I shared a room with this man unless I chose to tell. My moral reservations felt like clunky, unwanted furniture in my psychic living room, too cumbersome to live with but too heavy to move out.

The next morning, we shared coffee, omelets, and papaya on a round marble table with a view across the Malecón to the sea.

"How did you sleep?" I asked.

"Not well," Gary replied, matter-of-factly. "I was quite cold and I didn't have enough blankets." His response swept me with regret. If not for my rigid sense of propriety, I would have been close by, able to bring him extra covers during the night. And didn't "spooning" come from Ireland? For a moment, I imagined warmly enfolding his tiny body with my more generous one.

On the television in the breakfast room, the CNN newscaster announced that Afghan soldiers were being flown from Kandahar to the base at Guantánamo. I offered that it seemed like a perverse contradiction that our government could condemn Cuba for human rights violations and then house prisoners on Cuban soil in violation of their human rights. Gary agreed, and I felt pleased, as if I'd just shown him a good report card. The difference in our ages made him the perfect foil for such projections which surfaced randomly amid the more maternal impulses that his frailty evoked.

Through a wrought iron fence we watched Cubans walking by, wearing sweaters and jackets in this coolest month of the year. The sky was clear, but chilly winds blew in from the ocean, puffing up their garb. Chirping birds and groaning buses competed with voices from the television.

We finished breakfast. Gary called the guesthouse and wrote down the address. The doorman hailed a taxi. As I handed Gary his cane and offered my arm to help him to the cab, he muttered gruffly, "I'm not entirely helpless!"

"Certainly not," I thought, as his fingers slipped around my forearm.

The taxi pulled away, and I missed him immediately. Sure that he would have need of an able-bodied friend and eager to assist him in exchange for his company, I resolved to call him the next day.

With the morning to fill before meeting with my new landlord, I went walking. Just around the corner from the hotel, four men with sun-weathered faces and yesterday's whiskers were playing dominoes, their game framed by an arched overhang and blue pillars buffed to a soft matte finish by decades of salty sea breezes. The scene welcomed me back.

I lunched alone at an outdoor café, sheltered by a red and white awning and surrounded by tropical plants. A sprawl of slogans decked the walls, and I strained to translate them without my dictionary. *El pesimismo jamás ganó una batalla* (Pessimism never won a battle). *Todo es hermoso y constante, todo es música y razón y todo, cómo el diamante, antes que luz, es carbón* (Everything is handsome and constant, everything is music and reason, and, everything, like a diamond before light, is carbon). This was a café frequented by foreigners and I assumed these had been approved for tourist consumption, but oddly, they seemed addressed to long-suffering Cubans. Dosed with black beans, rice, and chicken, and cheered on by the signs, I returned to the hotel to await my soon-to-be landlord.

The sun was high when Ariel appeared on foot. With his thick glasses and pasty complexion, he looked more suited to the stacks of a library than the streets of Havana, but together we swiftly covered a dozen blocks on foot, winding through a congestion of pedestrians, bicycles, Moscow Ladas, and

Detroit Pontiacs. He set an impossibly swift pace and I struggled to keep up. With my laptop slung over my shoulder and sweat soaking my shirt, I tried as best I could to avoid the unexpected bump of brick or dip of pothole. Ariel didn't seem to share my preoccupation about tripping, hurriedly dragging my wheeled suitcase over the rutted streets.

When we turned onto Calle San Juan de Dios and approached what would be my new home, Ariel paused and took a breath. "By the way, last night I rented the apartment to eleven young *Argentinos*," he said. He sounded nonchalant, as if he were commenting on the weather. I stopped mid-step and he registered my look of alarm. "Not to worry," he assured, "just for last night." He had informed the group of students that they had to leave that day since I would be moving in. They just hadn't yet returned from their morning outing to collect their luggage. He had consolidated their belongings in the living room. My bedroom was ready, he assured, and I could put my things there until the Argentines returned to vacate the rest of the space. "*¡No hay problema!*" he repeated, with a bit of irritation.

We arrived at the landmark pile of rubble, passed through the entryway, and climbed the stairs past the bra factory to the apartment. Ariel unbolted the door and pushed it open. I stepped inside. The space where the sofa had been was now a floor-to-ceiling heap of backpacks and duffle bags. Clothes were strewn everywhere, some still damp and spread out on the furniture to dry. The kitchen was piled with unwashed dishes, donut cartons, a sack of *mate*, and what looked like an odd teapot for preparing the Argentine drink. I made my way through the debris to the bedroom in the back, thankful that it was clean and bare of all but furniture. Ariel stayed behind in the *sala*.

I was unpacking and hanging my clothes in the wardrobe, when I heard the ruckus of their arrival—all eleven of them. At the sight of what Ariel had done with their possessions, the yelling began. I stayed hidden and quiet and tried to decipher the barrage of accusations and retorts as male voices grew louder and louder. Between the speed of their speech and the swish of their accents, I could make out only fragments—"commitment.... *nos engañaron* (you deceived us).... no way!"—but I got the gist. The young men insisted that Ariel had promised them lodging for more than one night and was reneging on his promise. Ariel sharply denied this, but his attempts to defend himself sounded hollow. I pictured him shrinking in the face of the onslaught; his shoulders hunched forward, his chest concave. As the argument escalated, so did my anxiety. I feared that they might come to blows.

I surveyed the bedroom and bathroom. There was no escape without walking through the altercation. I was trapped. Flustered, I started stuffing my clothes back into the suitcase, thinking that one *norteamericana* should not displace eleven Argentines. Then, as quickly as the shouting began, it ceased, replaced by soft murmurs as the young people gathered their belongings and prepared to leave.

Ashamed of having inadvertently precipitated their eviction, I cracked open the bedroom door and cautiously stepped out, a box of peanut butter and chocolate Ohio buckeyes in my hand. At least I could sweeten their departure. To my surprise, there were several young women amidst the men; I had only picked out male voices in the commotion. At the sight of me, a fellow with auburn hair stepped forward and introduced himself. He must have discerned from my face or the box of candy in my hand that I was feeling squeamish about what had transpired, for he quickly volunteered that neither he nor his friends bore me any ill will.

"No, no, keep the chocolates," he insisted. "You will need them for another occasion." Then he turned the tables, waving me toward the kitchen. "Do you want some cake—or donuts—or some wine?" He swung open the refrigerator door and started pulling out leftovers, a large half-eaten confection covered with creamy frosting, some fruit, and a bottle of red wine. Apparently they had shared quite a fiesta the night before.

"*You're* not the problem," the young man continued. "*Ese hombre*, THAT man, he's the problem! And it's not the first time this has happened to us since we've been here." Several of his compatriots joined us in the kitchen and a lively repartee followed as the first man divided food and drink between what he could fit in his backpack and what he insisted on leaving for me. He and his friends recalled several other episodes when they had parted with more money than intended, and they broke into gales of laughter as stories were retold. Their month long vacation had been a financial fiasco from the start. The Argentine economy had collapsed shortly after their arrival, devaluing the money they had brought with them and making their losses all the more jolting. They too had felt vulnerable, trapped, and flustered.

The resilience of youth was in their laughter. *"¡Es Cuba!"* one man yelped. The room filled with smoke from their cigarettes and the soft Js of their accents. Only Ariel, the technical winner of the argument, seemed ill at ease. He sat silent in the corner, staring at the stereo system and waiting for the group to leave.

When the Argentines departed, I excused myself and returned to the task of unpacking, while I pondered the characters in this drama. Maybe Ariel's surface timidity covered a sociopathic streak. Or maybe the impossible Cuban economy made con men out of otherwise honest people. I thought about the young travelers, so verbally combative one moment and conciliatory the next. Where would the pack of them go and where would they sleep that night?

Emptying the outside pocket of my suitcase I found the copy of *Vanidades* that I had purchased in Cancun. The timing was perfect: Ariel was still licking his wounds in the living room and could use a lift. I emerged from the bedroom. "*Para usted*," I said, handing him the glossy rag. The sight of it cheered him; he broke into a smile and began to flip through the pages.

"*¡Mil gracias!*" he exclaimed. "Thanks to you, Rosa and I will be among the very first in the country to have the horoscopes for the New Year. I can't wait to find out what kind of year it will be."

Neither could I.

chapter 10

My new kitchen had few accoutrements. Poking in the empty cupboard, I realized that I would probably be eating on the streets rather than stocking it. The clanging and gurgling of water filling the tanks over the kitchen at dawn was disconcerting, but the view through the slatted bedroom windows was sublime: sandpaper buildings in putty and grey as far as I could see—a topsy-turvy of angles and edges worthy of Picasso. The sofa in the *sala* was comfortable enough for me to nestle there with papers and notebooks spread around me and contently tap away on my laptop. All in all, I was pleased with myself. I couldn't quite believe that I had made this happen—that by daring to make a few odd decisions, my life had become so rich.

From family to college dorm to married student housing, I had made each leap as if there were no other options. The thought of living on my own had never occurred to me until well after marriage. Then too-much-to-lose had forced the nascent urge into hibernation, only now to be stirred awake by Havana heat.

Just as he said he would, Ariel showed up on my first morning to fix me a simple breakfast of coffee, bread, and fluorescent pink yoghurt. He repeated that Rosita would find someone to do my laundry and that he would show me a dollar store nearby where I could buy food, but his manner was perfunctory and he didn't mention José Martí or any other poet. Instead, he announced that the fumigator would be stopping by to spray the apartment with "something toxic" to kill mosquitoes.

If Ariel would help me, I thought I would upgrade from ersatz refrigerator banking to a real account where I could leave surplus funds between trips. *"No hay problema,"* Ariel assured. With fourteen hundred dollars in bills tucked in my money belt, I followed him a few blocks to an international bank, a cavernous stone structure with a pretentious pillared façade that suggested big money and flusher times. Under the vaulted ceiling, a teller devoted to handling *divisa* (hard currency) carefully examined each bill that I handed her to make sure it wasn't counterfeit. A half-hour of paper shuffling later, I held a red plastic passbook in my hand, like the one I'd received as a teenager after opening a right-of-passage savings account. This one, my first off-shore account, gave me an adolescent sense of naughtiness. I had no idea if I was violating some obscure regulation of my government, and I didn't care.

~

By late afternoon I'd had enough self-sufficiency for one day. I called Gary, my elderly friend, and offered to stop by. He sounded delighted. He would welcome my visit, some leisure after his full day of interviewing religious and community leaders.

The next few evenings, we ate supper together at his guesthouse, a capacious cream-colored residence with a large front porch. Over nondescript soups, *congrí*, and occasional scraps of meat, we shared the events of our days and became better acquainted. I learned that Gary's expertise encompassed Latin America, human rights, Catholicism, poverty, social justice, and international politics. He was a man of words, fluent in five languages, and liked to reminisce about his travels as much as I liked to reminisce about mine. After supper, he and I would walk in mincing steps to his dorm-like room where he would sit on a hardback chair and I on the edge of the bed while we talked further. He had a penchant for piercing lighter conversation with pointed questions or spontaneous mentoring.

"Why do you go by Juanita?" he asked. "Certainly it's not because you are diminutive!" he mused. I smarted at this oblique reference to my plumpness. "That was the name given to me by Nicaraguans when I was young and in the Peace Corps," I replied, trying not to show my embarassment. He shifted his tack, pushing me to justify myself in another arena.

"What is a woman like you *doing* in Cuba?" he asked, looking at me intensely, his bushy eyebrows pulled together in question. It was a query I thought I had already answered on the flight from Cancun. "I want to learn about Cuban health care and write," I said for the second time, feeling defensive. My answer seemed to fall short of what he was asking and seemed a bit off to me too.

"So you want to write?" he repeated, as if settling for an answer that would have to do for now. "If what you want to do is write, then let me show you how a journalist prepares for a working trip." He pulled out a spiral notebook and flipped it open. I was relieved to see that his notes looked remarkably similar to my own—jottings about books, websites, people, and places. Maybe I wasn't too far behind.

"What do you want to write?" he asked, and I told him about the research study that Enrique and I hoped to do. "I want to be able to tell stories about how the embargo affects real people. If we get to interview doctors and patients about the stresses they experience because of the embargo, I should have plenty of material." I recounted the trip to MINSAP that I had made that afternoon, one more cordial interaction with the kindly Dr. Portilla who had had no news to share on our proposal, still under consideration. Exasperated at the prospect of more of same, I told Gary of my repeated ever-agreeable but frustrating encounters with state officials and the advice I had been given to persist in my efforts. Gary looked thoughtful. "I've learned that three yeses usually means no." The intelligence of his words would sink in later.

Between Gary's perspicacious probes and enigmatic statements, I asked him more about himself. At first he made me work hard to elicit information. "You can Google me when you get home," he said, with a glint in his eye. But with each evening visit he became less reticent, reminding me of my psychotherapy practice and the natural loosening of disclosure that springs from a comfortable relationship. In his presence, my boundaries were loosening too. I no longer declined his offers of Scotch.

Gary had grown up in rural Ireland and had been educated in a one-room schoolhouse. He had been required to memorize one entire

Shakespearian play each year, and whole sections of text were still lodged firmly in his mind. He was the son of a solicitor who helped citizens charged with crimes such as having illegal Gaelic rather than Irish words written on the sides of their donkey carts. For eleven years he had prepared for the priesthood but been denied ordination at the final hour without explanation. He thought that perhaps he had been too inquisitive, but in the absence of knowledge about how the decision was made, he hesitated to call it unfair.

Blocked from the priesthood, he had become a journalist, married, earned a doctorate in Spanish literature and a law degree, pursued international business based in New York, raised a son, written for *Life*, *Look*, *Time,* and various leftist magazines, and travelled five continents, writing all the while. He had authored over thirty books, several about the papacy and many about Latin America. Later I would read that he was considered the pre-eminent Catholic journalist of the twentieth century.

His wife had died a number of years earlier, more than a decade after suffering a devastating stroke. Her care had depleted his savings. In recent years, his travels—limited only slightly by his health and diminishing stamina—were typically covered by whoever was paying him to write. He lived on his Social Security income of about ten thousand dollars a year, supplemented by about five thousand dollars from writing jobs.

"That's terrible!" I exclaimed, thinking that he deserved more than poverty after a life of such accomplishment.

"No it's not!" he admonished harshly. "I can do whatever I *want* on that!" I cringed, thinking of the generous stash I had just deposited in the bank.

Our conversations were zigzags of verbal forays, unexpected turns, and occasional dead-ends. In a single conversation, Gary would lapse into Latin, quote verse after verse from *The Merchant of Venice,* recount details of his childhood homework assignments, chide me for a mispronunciation, and launch into a diatribe against the U.S. government. "Trash and abandon," he declared, referring to one Central American country or another. His voice trembled with indignation. "That is what we do everywhere. Trash and abandon!" He was strongly identified with liberation theology and, in the 1980s, had helped found the sanctuary movement for sheltering refugees from Central America. His home was in San Antonio, Texas, where he held an open house for his friends every Saturday night when he was at home. "Maybe you can come sometime."

I listened in amazement. His life had embraced a multitude of interests and had stretched from Ireland to Texas with the whole world in between.

"How did you end up in San Antonio?" I asked.

"I didn't *end up* anywhere!" he retorted sternly.

His response made me pause. Gary still saw his life as an ongoing process with final chapters yet to be written. He was still doing important work. He was still planning occasions to enjoy his friends and was willing to expand his circle to include me. Meanwhile, I was feeling sorry for myself for mere middle age. My dread about seeing sixty on the not-distant-enough horizon felt preposterous.

On Sunday, Gary invited me to accompany him to services at the Ebenezer Baptist Church next to the Martin Luther King Center where he had been conducting his interviews. Though attending church was not part of my regular routine, I said yes, thinking my presence might make his outing easier. He could lean on me and I could help him in and out of taxis.

I hadn't thought much about religion in Cuba, and before meeting Gary I had assumed that Catholicism and Afro-Cuban *santería* were the only religious practices with much following. From him I learned that Protestant denominations were flourishing too, and although few in number, Jews had both a synagogue and a kosher grocery store in Havana. Any preconception that communism and religion didn't mix was dispelled by one morning with the Baptists.

The pale yellow Ebenezer Baptist Church sits close to the street in a busy neighborhood of Maríanao. The Sunday service was packed with a preponderance of grey- and white-haired folks. Women outnumbered men by two or three to one. The women were in dresses, the men clean-shaven. It was already hot outside, but thick walls and suspended electric fans kept us cool.

The service was lively and egalitarian. This Sunday's preacher was a woman and God was referred to as "our Mother/Father." Visiting students from a U.S. seminary sang in English and Spanish, accompanied by tambourines and bursts of clapping. One of the students spoke, asserting, "Jesus is bigger than politics, government, race, or gender." In an interlude devoted to greeting others, my cheeks were pleasantly smeared with kisses. I was comforted by the hospitality of the congregation, the inclusiveness of the language, the presence of young and old, healthy and infirm, and people of every color. It didn't matter that I was neither Baptist nor Cuban or that I couldn't read the hymnal fast enough to sing along. And in the embrace of the occasion, it felt just right to have a frail old religious radical holding the crook of my arm.

The congregation lingered after the service to share coffee in the courtyard next to the church. As we streamed out of the sanctuary, a zaftig woman with a round face pushed through the crowd to greet me. "*¡Venceremos!*" she said exuberantly, hugging me and planting a kiss on my cheek. We will overcome. What? I wondered, sin, racism, the embargo? I had no idea, but responded with equal enthusiasm, *"¡Sí! ¡Juntas venceremos!"* Yes, together we shall overcome.

Gary and I downed coffee from tiny white paper cups under the giant face of Cesar Chávez, part of a mural painted by Pastors for Peace, a group from the United States that openly defied OFAC regulations by regularly bringing humanitarian donations to Cuba without asking for permission. *"Sí, se puede romper el bloqueo,"* the mural declared. Yes, you can break the blockade.

Although this was the only time I attended with Gary, the Ebenezer Baptist Church became a place to which I returned by myself on several occasions. I felt anchored there in a community that welcomed all comers. The sanctuary was true to its name, a place where I felt neither the blockade nor the divide of politics and culture. When I returned alone, I always missed Gary's scruffy white-haired presence standing next to me, hymnal in hand.

Going to church with Gary didn't alter my religious beliefs, but knowing him as a person pushed me in a contemplative direction. He appeared at a point in my life when I needed spiritual mentoring even if I didn't know it. His thoughtful calm and unflagging commitment to social justice and human rights made me want to partake of whatever spiritual nectars nourished him.

For the week Gary was in Havana, I spent my days within the triangle formed by my apartment, MINSAP, and the guest house in Vedado. One evening, tired and anticipating that my visit with Gary would be short, I flagged a cab in the Parque Central. My *taxista* was named Fidel, the first Fidel I had met. I asked him to take me to the guesthouse and wait for me. When I arrived, Gary was bursting to tell me about his day. His eyes twinkled and then disappeared into the folds of his cheeks, "Today I interviewed Juan Valdéz, a *real* Juan Valdéz. I know that the other one was a fake because *I made him up*!" he said, boyish with glee

What was he talking about? I was perplexed until he reminded me of the old commercial that featured a Colombian coffee picker standing among the plants inspecting individual beans. His name had been Juan Valdéz. Gary explained that, in one of his many careers, he had headed the public relations office for the Colombian Coffee Federation that had invented the character. Each conversation revealed another facet of Gary's lengthy and jam-packed life, leaving me wondering what would come next.

When I was ready to return to my apartment, I found Fidel relaxing on the front porch, smoking a cigarette. His left foot was balanced on his knee, exposing the sole of his shoe, fissured through in several places and falling apart in large disparate chunks.

I climbed into the back of the cab. The state of his shoe prompted me to ask Fidel how he made ends meet. Did he drive a cab all the time? No, he replied. He was an ironsmith by day, earning just two hundred pesos a month. To supplement his salary, he rented the cab he was driving from a doctor for five dollars an evening and then worked late into the night to find enough customers to make a profit.

"¡Es duro!" Fidel said, in a variant of *"No es fácil."* "If you saw the inside of my refrigerator right now, you would see that there is only water." He shook his head in resigned disbelief. "Imagine! The doctor can't live on what *he* earns either, so he has to rent me his car!" Hearing such a perfect example of the absurdity of Cuban economics gave me guilty pleasure. I didn't know what to do with such pearls, but I loved adding them to my collection.

I paid Fidel in dollars before disappearing into the dark stairwell that led up to my apartment. I took a tepid shower to remove the brine of the day and threw on my nightgown, while thinking about the hours I had just spent and the people I had just enjoyed. As staunchly independent as I saw myself to be and as much as I thought that I was becoming more introverted with age, the truth was more complex. I felt most alive in the company of others. I lay down between the cellophane sheets and turned off the light on the bed-side table. I was alone but content. The music of social encounters—in the streets, on the rooftops, from the dilapidated buildings all round—slipped through the slats of my windows.

chapter 11

The sidewalk was clean, dry, and smooth and it was broad daylight, but I slipped anyway, right in front of the Club de Amistad where I was going to meet Gary. Trying to avoid a fall, I staggered forward, propelled horizontally until all was lost and I landed hard, my right arm outstretched on the cement. The pain was immediate and severe. Stunned, hurt, and with blood dripping from my forearm, I sat frozen on the pavement, incredulous that, with all the street hazards of Havana that I had so carefully avoided, I could have fallen *here.* Dazed, I struggled to my feet, cradling my right arm with my left, and sought help at the Friendship Club.

The woman at the front desk dropped her jaw at the sight of me, and her alarmed expression triggered a flood of tears that I had contained until that moment. She offered me a seat, found alcohol and cotton to clean my wound, and provided a gauze pad to staunch the bleeding. I later learned that such gauze was in exceedingly short supply.

I was still reeling in pain and trying to recover my equilibrium when Gary arrived, surprised and concerned but exuding his customary calm. Although I'd known him for just five days, at that moment he was my oldest and dearest friend.

My shoulder throbbed and I sheltered my arm against my body, worried that something was broken. Several years earlier, in eagerness to enjoy the

Piazza di San Marco before the heat of the day, I had tumbled down the stairs of a Venetian hotel and landed hand-first on the stone floor. Not wanting to become entangled with health insurance claims in a foreign country, I had skipped seeing a doctor and nursed pain for weeks, only to discover upon returning home that my wrist had been fractured. It was a mistake I was determined not to make a second time.

In Cuba health insurance would be irrelevant; financially I was on my own. Even in my distraught state, I knew that a door of opportunity had been thrown open. I may have missed the chance to have my tooth drilled by Norberto's dentist, but I could still grab this chance to be cared for by Cuban physicians. I looked at Gary. His presence reassured. A circle of Cubans formed around us and I saw compassion in their faces.

"I think I need to go to a hospital," I said, regaining my composure. "Is there a place where Cubans go that would see me?"

Someone in the gathering mentioned the emergency room of the Hospital Ortopédico Fructuosa Rodríguez. It was close and the preeminent center for orthopedic care. "Since this happened to you here and you weren't injured before you arrived, they should take you." My distress was eased by the amusing thought that exclusions for pre-existing condition were not unique to capitalism.

"I'll go with you," said Gary, the man I had thought so needed *me.*

Someone in the swarm called a cab. Someone else produced a bag of ice that I balanced on my shoulder with my good hand. When the taxi arrived, the driver looked conflicted as to whom he should assist, the feeble old man with the cane or the disheveled younger woman with the bloody arm and the ice bag. Many hands helped both of us. Settled in the back seat next to Gary, I relaxed, knowing I did not have to cope with this alone. So much for who was going to help whom—with a momentary stumble of a sandaled foot, I had tripped into neediness.

The taxi pulled up to a somber two-story structure that looked to be made of solid cement. Large eyes of windows were lidded with closed wooden blinds giving the appearance that the hospital was asleep. We were left under the cement overhang at the entrance to the emergency room. We walked slowly into a shabby waiting area where dozens of people eyed us curiously from hard wooden chairs. We must have looked like a May-

December pair who had hit the skids of injury on a Cuba vacation. No one in the waiting room looked like a foreigner until Gary sat down among the others to wait while I sought treatment.

Half of the ceiling was missing, exposing a skeleton of bare pipes and wires. A patient treatment area was blocked from view with sheets of green plastic suspended from metal frames. I joined the line in front of a desk where a woman was recording names of new patients. When my turn came, she skipped that formality and sent me to a side room where a nurse firmly informed me that I needed to be seen at a clinic devoted to visitors from abroad. That I had been injured on Cuban soil made no difference. A co-worker called us another taxi, and Gary and I were soon riding to the Clínica Ciro García in Playa.

We were left at a pristine white stucco entrance that contrasted starkly with that of the dreary hospital we had just left. The bright entry hall was decorated with soft pastel paintings of the usual three: José Martí, Che Guevara, and Fidel Castro. The almost empty waiting room was furnished with simply upholstered but cushy black chairs. Gary settled into one.

I approached the receptionist. There was no line. She requested my name and passport information and within three minutes I was whisked into a spotless exam room where a male nurse scrubbed the contusion on my arm and painted it with an orange antiseptic, skipping the bandage that I expected to cover the open wound. Then he escorted me to a comfortably furnished office where, under large sunny windows, I waited for the doctor.

In no time the doctor appeared. He was just shy of movie-set handsome with abundant white hair that matched his coat. He introduced himself in English as Dr. Corona, a specialist in rehabilitation medicine. Perfect, I thought, given that I'd been injured. He asked me what had happened and how old I was, but took no medical history, although I volunteered that I had chronic tendonitis in the same shoulder that I had injured. He examined my arm, moving it carefully. He asked me what hurt and noted when I winced. He was soft-spoken, his manner avuncular, and our conversation see-sawed between languages since he was as eager to speak English as I was to speak Spanish.

He needed to take an X-ray to rule out a fracture. A woman appeared and took me to the radiology area while Dr. Corona trailed closely behind.

The doctor himself positioned me on the examining table and, as the technician took the picture, I could see him pacing back and forth in the anteroom, waiting for the result as if nothing were more important to him than the state of my health. Five minutes passed. The picture was ready. He clipped it to the light-board and together we looked— there was no fracture.

"Have you ever had your shoulder injected?" he asked. "Once," I replied. "Don't do it again," he said firmly, pointing to a spot on the film that suggested some decalcification.

He led me back to his office and we sat down. He shared his conclusion that my injuries were only to soft tissues, but that I needed to be careful in tending them lest my tendonitis worsen. For the next few days I should use a sling and intermittent ice packs. He offered me no medicine for pain. Perhaps he had none. "And you need to take daily doses of the Cuban sun— once in the morning before ten o'clock and again in the afternoon, after four." Yeah, yeah, I thought, my shoulder throbbing. For what conditions wouldn't that be good advice?

Dr. Corona accompanied me to the clinic pharmacy to get a sling. When they didn't have one the right size, he led me to the entrance of the clinic and pointed to an international pharmacy across the street. "Just don't go to the national pharmacies," he advised, "They won't have any."

Our consult was over and I reached out to shake his hand. He leaned over and kissed me on the cheek—Cuban style. Nice touch, I thought. Did communists conduct market research to figure out what makes for customer satisfaction? Behind a glass partition a woman calculated my bill: twenty-five dollars for the consultation and twenty-five dollars for the film, payable in dollars only.

In the chair where I had left him, Gary had dozed off like a cat in sunshine. He looked so blissful that I didn't want to disturb him, so I crossed the street to the pharmacy alone, only to discover that they didn't have any slings at all. *"No se preocupe,"* the pharmacist explained. He would get me to a location that would have one. He dashed outside and hailed a cab that was parked nearby, apparently part of the coordinated care in place for tourists. I returned to the waiting room and reluctantly wakened Gary. We were taken to a German-Cuban orthopedic supplies facility where, after passing under another portrait of Che, I was greeted by another affable doctor who took measurements for a custom-fitted sling. He charged me fifteen dollars, *"el mínimo."*

During my brief spell as a patient, there were no questions about my financial situation before I was given care, and I was attended to promptly and with compassion. But what impressed me most was that I was never left alone for more than a minute or two. This was not like home. I passed not a moment in a cold examining room in a paper gown waiting for help to materialize. I was given unrushed and focused attention at every station of the process. The pampering felt like salve on the emotional wounds of the trauma.

Nevertheless the experience reminded me of shopping for silk in India where, if you ask to see a piece of cloth, a dozen men rush to take one bolt down from the shelf and roll it out for display. While the continuity of care was impressive, shouldn't the doctors have had something better to do than treat me so solicitously? Couldn't people of lesser training have filled their roles more economically? Maybe I was just so jaded by the fragmented and impersonal encounters that pass for health care in the States that I was disconcerted by the immediate and sensitive response to my needs.

And of course I kept wondering how my care would have been different had I been a Cuban and provided treatment through the emergency room at Fructuosa Rodríguez. Just because the building was shabby and the waiting room was full of people, I couldn't conclude that treatment there would have been inferior, could I? After all, this was Cuba, known throughout world for its health care system, for the number and dedication of its physicians, and for its impressive health statistics. The fact that I had been shunted into a facility just for tourists led me to conclusions I preferred to resist: that health care on the island came in two versions, only one of which was deemed appropriate for foreign consumption.

A visit to MINSAP on a steamy afternoon with my shoulder aching and my arm in a sling evoked the usual noncommittal response. I was discouraged. Gary, by contrast, looked tired but happy after days of productive interviewing. I was jealous. He seemed so wise and self-possessed, while I was floundering.

"What do you know now that you didn't know when you were younger?" I asked him one evening. The Scotch was warming my gullet and erasing all vestiges of pain. "You have to learn to roll with the punches," he replied. "And not take everything so seriously."

His response hit me like a fist. Maybe I was taking our research project too seriously. What would "rolling with the punches" look like for me if MINSAP approval never materialized? Could I—just maybe—relax and trust that I could find my way in Cuba without the structure of a sanctioned research project? If I were lucky, maybe surprise opportunities could fill in the blanks. I thought of another tidbit that my philosophical friend had shared, gleaned from six decades of contact with this peculiar country: "In Cuba everything is prohibited and everything is done." With pluck, maybe I could assume a more Cuban perspective—break a few rules or at least test the limits.

I thought about just letting loose and writing about my personal experience of Cuba. For several years, I'd been skirting the edges of creative writing without fully plunging in. I allowed myself to imagine becoming a writer and relinquishing my university position. I was shocked by the audacity of my thoughts, their appeal, and then the wave of anxiety that followed.

I shared with Gary my fear that, as weary as I was of my academic life, I might not—already in my mid fifties—be able to chart a new direction for myself. Gary's face lengthened as he listened. He looked at me as seriously as if I had announced a terminal illness. I thought I saw sadness in his eyes.

"Juanita, you are *young*, you have your whole life ahead of you." It was a cliché. But coming from this wizened old leprechaun the words were license to count the years between us as a gift that I might be given, to do with as I chose. We lapsed into thoughtful quiet while sharing a nip of Scotch from the liter bottle that occupied the space in his suitcase a lesser person might have used for an extra set of clothes.

With his journalistic mission complete, Gary left Cuba on schedule. I didn't want to say goodbye. He had more wisdom that I still craved, but which was impossible to extract in a rush. I knew that I might never see him again—even if he hadn't told me about the aortic aneurysm that was ominously growing inside him. When he slipped himself into yet one more taxi cab, his *despedida* felt a bit hurried, as if he didn't want to see my tears.

I nursed my shoulder with care for the rest of my January stay. The waiters in the patio of the Hotel Nacional didn't seem to mind bringing me bags of ice as long as I occasionally ordered a ham and cheese sandwich. The prescribed daily doses of sunshine weren't a problem either, although walking to and from MINSAP through the barrios of Central Havana was probably not quite what Dr. Corona had in mind. Occasionally I splurged on a massage. For twenty to thirty dollars, less than half of what I would pay at home but the equivalent of a physician's monthly salary in Cuba, I could stretch out on a massage table in a private room at the Hotel Riviera. There Jorge, the hotel physician, would energetically rub me down, his whole body vibrating and sweating with the effort. Convinced that my shoulder pain was bursitis, he applied magnets and poked me with funny metal gizmos in a healing ritual that only he understood. Sometimes the pummeling evoked paroxysms of pain, but it was only after returning to Ohio that I understood why.

When I was finally able to see my regular doctor at home, he ordered more tests. Fifteen hundred dollars of MRI and X-rays later, an orthopedic surgeon informed me that my arm was fractured close to the shoulder and I had a torn rotator cuff. Luckily, the bones were healing in place, although I would need physical therapy before my next trip.

Curious, I handed the surgeon the X-ray that Dr. Corona had taken in Havana and asked him to examine it. He held it up to the light. The quality of the picture was fine, he said, and although he thought he could discern the fracture, he couldn't be certain and he had the advantage of knowing it was there. "The problem was not with the film," he concluded. "The problem was that just one picture was taken. A fracture should never be ruled out based on a single view."

In Cuba, both X-ray film and the chemical reagents necessary for developing images were in short supply due to the U.S. embargo of medical sales to the island. Obviously, such scarcities were shaping medical care even in their showcase clinics for foreigners. For the first time in my life, I contemplated the possibility that I—a citizen of the United States—had been directly and adversely affected by my country's foreign policy.

How much worse must be the effects of the embargo on those without recourse to an alternate resource-rich system—Cubans without relatives or friends abroad to provide needed drugs and medical supplies not available in Cuba. I wished that my empathy could have been born of other means—without falling, without breaking bones, without pain. But then, I might have missed the reminder that who needs help and who gives help can reverse in an instant, that self-sufficiency is at best a temporary state.

chapter 12

My diligent visits to MINSAP were generating nothing new. Each time I passed by the mural in the lobby, I dreaded what I knew would come next: another round of vague evasions and put-offs by Dr. Portilla. "Yes, your proposal is being considered" began to sound like "Don't hold your breath." Maybe Gary was right about the three yeses.

The glacial speed and non-response of MINSAP was nudging me to jettison my initial aspirations. Whenever my shoulder twinged, I was reminded of what I had learned as a patient, an education that had nothing to do with an officially sanctioned project. By mobilizing my observational and interpersonal skills and using loose qualitative methods, I thought I could learn as much and enjoy myself more than if I rigidly adhered to my earlier plans. Instead of writing a paper for a social science journal, maybe I could write a magazine article or a book—more narrative than science.

That I do "research" was required by the Office of Foreign Assets Control, and contemplating any change in plans stirred up concerns about being charged with violating the U.S. travel restrictions. But beyond OFAC fears lay more personal anxieties. Relinquishing the project, I would later realize, represented a psychological shift away from my father's hard science orientation and toward my mother's softer way of being in the world—more participatory and journalistic. The shift was overdue and emotionally complicated. I had spent too many years sharing my father's academic world for it to be otherwise.

Whatever I chose to do, I would still need to jump through the hoops of OFAC regulations to maintain my legitimacy in future trips. Unless I found another reason to travel on humanitarian license—unlikely if our project wasn't approved—I would have to keep a schedule that I could justify as "full-time research." Thankfully, cultural immersion coupled with observation and recording was considered appropriate methodology within the tradition of anthropology and was gaining credibility within other social sciences. I decided that if MINSAP didn't give our project the go-ahead, I would claim this approach as my own and hope to generate experiences worthy of the risk.

Sitting with Enrique in his tiny *sala* was a soothing break that I often sought. Sometimes we just sat quietly and watched Fidel on the evening news. He always seemed to be mixing with ordinary folks in crisis, praising their virtues and encouraging their revolutionary zeal. Other times, over Belkis' coffee, we commiserated about our lack of progress at MINSAP. As time dragged on, Enrique sensed that I needed diversion while we awaited definitive judgment.

"How about a visit to a leprosy sanatorium?" he asked one evening. He relished issuing such unexpected invitations. I brightened, surprised that such a place existed in Cuba and intrigued at the possibility of a firsthand look. What could be more enticing than an exotic disease that I had only read about in books, coupled with the opportunity to explore how the embargo shaped the lives of patients in such an institution? I pushed for details. On the grounds of the leprosy sanatorium in the village of El Rincón stood a convent that housed a dozen Sisters of Charity who cared for the lepers in coordination with personnel from MINSAP. The Mother Superior was a childhood friend of Enrique's and he had spoken with her to arrange our visit.

Early the next morning, we boarded Enrique's Moskavitch for the trip to El Rincón, about thirty kilometers from Havana. We left town via the Plaza of the Revolution and passed the spot beneath the looming image of Che where, in 1998, the Pope had blessed the Cuban masses. The Catholic associations made me think of Gary. I missed him and wished that he could share this excursion with me. We curved around the monument to José Martí, passed the building that housed the offices of *El Comandante*, and headed toward the airport.

I gazed out the window at the road, peppered with political propaganda. Every vertical surface along this highway of hellos and goodbyes seemed to be covered with the verbal effluvia of the Committee of Revolutionary Orientation. The signs looked homemade. Words painted in dark blue, red, and grey accompanied images of the usual three heroes: Che, Fidel, and José Martí.

I lapsed into trance with the rhythmic repetition of slogans parading by:

"Merge with this virtuous time."

"43 Years of Triumphal Revolution!"

"Always Rebel!"

"There is no greater honor than to be a combatant for human health."

"¡Hasta la victoria siempre!" Toward Victory Always! It was the hackneyed mantra of the Cuban revolution. Seeing the words pleasurably aroused my anti-imperialist sentiments, as if Che and I shared a secret. Although I never knew what victory we were so fervently striving for, I had come to feel part of the struggle.

Beyond Havana's urban sprawl and the airport, the propaganda signs all but disappeared as we entered agricultural terrain. After so much time in the city, I delighted in the green foliage of plantains and kapok trees and experimental horticulture plots. We passed through the village of Santiago de Las Vegas with its AIDS sanatorium. It was a regular stop on the tour circuit for foreign medical delegations and one I had made on my first trip to Cuba, a trip that now seemed long ago. I had learned that, in spite of having forced quarantine on AIDS patients early in the epidemic, Cuba had established a positive international reputation in the prevention and control of the disease and had the lowest rate of infection in Latin America. The sanatorium was now used mainly for temporary care and the education of newly diagnosed patients. Our destination, the leprosarium, was a few kilometers beyond.

El Rincón was not a pretty town. It strung out for half a mile along a two-lane road. Simple houses of stucco and wood stood close to the curb, some with enclosed front gardens and others with porches exposed to the street. The village consisted of little more than a scattering of houses, the hospital sanatorium complex surrounded by a stone wall, and the large red-roofed Church of San Lázaro.

Passing the church, we pulled up to an iron gate where a guard sat in a covered enclosure. I noticed that several men milling nearby were missing limbs or fingers.

"We are here to see *Sor* Carmen," Enrique said to the guard, using the honorary appellation for a Catholic sister. *"Adelante,"* the man replied and waved us forward through the gate. We came to a stop facing a handsome stone building. White iron chairs sat on the well-maintained front portico. Standing at the door waiting for a response to our knocks, I looked around. The convent was surrounded by the deteriorated buildings of the leprosarium that looked like they had not seen fresh paint since before the revolution.

Sor Carmen welcomed us and led us into a gracious salon, beyond which casual guests were not permitted. Although I was wary of organized religion and its emissaries, I liked Sor Carmen the moment I met her. She was a young mother superior, in her thirties, short and compactly curved with a little double chin. Her snug tan wimple framed her round cheeks and drew attention to her soulful, expressive eyes. Even within the confines of her habit, she carried herself with a lightness that suggested that she may have seen it all but still found reason to smile.

The three of us sat in dark wooden chairs in the cool room and Sor Carmen told me a bit about the sanatorium. It had been founded in Havana in 1847 and moved to El Rincón in 1916. There were about a hundred and fifty long-term adult residents and a smaller number who were considered transient even though some stayed seven or eight years. Many remained long after their illnesses were under control because the community had become their own, a place where they were less stigmatized than in the towns from which they had come. To be close to ill loved ones, some families moved to El Rincón from distant reaches of the county.

This was the country's only center for leprosy treatment. Cuba had met the goals of the World Health Organization for the control of the disease.

The residents of the sanatorium represented the residual cases in a country of eleven million people where the disease had been all but eradicated. New cases occasionally appeared but usually were successfully treated by neighborhood family doctors early in the disease process. Among the patients at the sanatorium were several married couples who had entered the facility together and lived in cottages on the grounds. One man and woman had met as patients and were married by the local priest. The Sisters of Charity—most of whom were nurses too—had been providing care to the lepers since 1854. They now functioned in cooperation with the state which supported the physicians who worked at the sanatorium and the dermatology hospital on the grounds.

My images of leprosy had been formed by old movies and avid reading of an illustrated medical text that I found on the family bookshelves when I was too young to be anything but appalled by the pictures. I wanted to know what kind of deformities I needed to brace for but couldn't bring myself to make such a question explicit.

"No one knows how the disease passes from one person to another," Sor Carmen explained. Some said it was contagious but only to susceptible people, perhaps those at a critical point in their physical development. Heredity was implicated by the clustering of cases in families, but the genetic component was hard to disentangle from shared living conditions. More men than women suffered from the disease and no one knew why. Most patients died not of leprosy but of secondary complications of treatment including renal and heart problems. Contrary to popular belief, leprosy was not easy to catch. After more than a hundred years of providing care, not a single nun had contracted the disease, though they were always careful to wash their hands after touching patients.

Sor Carmen introduced us to a tall dark physician in a worn white coat. He worked at the dermatology hospital that served both residents of the leprosarium and patients suffering from serious skin diseases sent to his facility from all over Cuba. "Do you experience any difficulties related to scarce medical supplies?" I asked.

"¿Sí, cómo no?" he replied. Often they cared for their patients without surgical gloves, antiseptics, analgesics, gauze, or replacement parts for rehabilitation equipment. Only one of the two surgery suites in the hospital was

functional because equipment was lacking to furnish the second. Most residents were elderly and, without materials to make dental prosthetics many found it painful or difficult to eat, forced to chew without dentures or with poorly fitting ones.

The drugs recommended by the World Health Organization to treat leprosy were available but often caused secondary problems such as ulcers, especially among patients afflicted with other diseases. Sadly, the drugs needed to address the common side effects of treatment were not available. Consequently, some patients stopped complying with the necessary medical regime after discharge and then had to return to the facility when skin lesions reappeared.

"With little, we try to resolve many things here," the doctor offered, sounding tired, but when he learned that I worked in a medical school, he perked up. Might I be able to help them access analgesics? Any assistance at all would be appreciated. *"Aun una aspirina alivia un dolor,"* he said. Even one aspirin alleviates a pain.

"Perhaps I could help— next time I come," I offered. In the face of such want, I couldn't say less, although I had no idea what I could actually do. Shipping supplies wasn't even an option because of the embargo, and my suitcase was miniscule relative to the size of their need.

The doctor took us on a walking tour of the facilities and grounds. As I looked around their scantily supplied microbiology lab, a technician shrugged her shoulders in resignation. "We do everything with love here," she said. Love, I thought, a poor substitute for chemicals and equipment to perform basic laboratory studies.

The patients were housed in the grim buildings I had first noticed, six or eight free-standing pavilions constructed in the early 1800s. From the outside, the buildings looked as unfit for habitation as those of state mental hospitals in the States where I had worked in graduate school. However, what I saw when we peeked inside one of them was reassuring. It was clean and generously accommodated twenty patients, each with a bed, rocking chair and bureau. Beyond the large pavilions, dilapidated stucco cottages for married couples were spaced along walkways under shade trees.

We ambled past a large group of men playing dominoes around a table in the sunshine. I couldn't keep from looking for what might not be there—

fingers, limbs, earlobes—simultaneously drawn to and repulsed by the prospects. Visible evidence of their disease was scant: some misshapen appendages and a few pug-noses from the collapse of facial cartilage. Many of the men were unshaven, and several held cigarettes where teeth should have been. They reminded me of the veterans that linger in the hallways of VA Hospitals at home. Sor Carmen engaged each resident in a friendly exchange as we walked by.

"Would you like to meet the hospital psychologist?" Sor Carmen asked me. *"¡Claro que sí!"* I replied, eager to meet one of my own kind. We climbed a narrow sidewalk to a flat stucco building where the psychologist had his "office," a three walled room with one side permanently open to the elements. There Sor Carmen introduced Enrique and me to a good-looking man in his sixties. His demeanor was kindly and quiet, and his French last name and ebony skin made me think he was of Haitian origin. He moved with an awkward gait and his fingers were blunted from leprosy. Enrique mentioned later that the disease and not his profession had probably brought him to this place.

My Cuban colleague offered us chairs in his open-air office. Under a shelf holding a sepia photo of Fidel and piles of tattered books and papers, he sat at his desk facing us. He proudly showed us several certificates documenting his achievements in—of all things—palmistry. He described ten studies he had conducted that supported the value of reading palms, comparing diagnoses derived from palmistry with those derived from more conventional assessment tools, including the Cattell 16PF Personality Inventory, an instrument that I had used in my doctoral research. He had initially learned palmistry from a North American acupuncturist and had developed his expertise further through reading. At first this work had been rejected, he explained, but more recently it had been recognized *"por todo el país,"* throughout the whole country. I stalled at some internal crossroads where my pride in the science of my profession threatened to collide with my cross-cultural tolerance. The best I could do was to divert us both by asking him to describe what being a psychologist at the leprosarium entailed.

He had worked at the sanatorium for more than thirty years. He interviewed all patients, took their psychosocial histories, and sometimes read their palms. Through these means he diagnosed each as normal, neurotic, or suffering from situational disturbances. For patients whose illness had resulted in social rejection, he sometimes provided individual psychotherapy. He also treated patients with skin diseases other than leprosy, such as psoriasis and plantar warts, which he treated successfully with hypnosis. I had no trouble believing that, remembering an obscure study I had read on the efficacy of hypnotherapy for treating warts.

Everything but the palm-reading was familiar to me from my own professional repertoire, but not nearly as intriguing. My skepticism didn't keep me from wanting to sample his perceptive talents. "Would you read my palms?" I asked.

He gently took my hands in his. Tracing lines with his misshapen fingers, he looked at them closely before he spoke. "There is cardiovascular risk on both your mother's side and your father's side," he noted, examining each hand. "And you are bad in business." Not having an entrepreneurial bone in my body, I expected he was right on the business front but my family had remarkably little heart trouble.

"And another thing," he added, "You have a personality that is *fuerte.*" Strong. No kidding, I thought. How many foreign women had found their way to his office?

Then he posed three questions to assess how neurotic I was.

"Do your hands get cold often?"

"No."

"Do they sweat often?"

"No."

"Do you bite your nails?"

"Well, sometimes."

I was relieved to have only one yes out of three. Even so, I suspected that he knew that I was more neurotic than his test indicated and was just too polite to say.

His earnestness and the tenderness of his touch dispelled the embarrassment I had initially felt at his unscientific approach. I imagined that even within the medium of palm reading there was healing validity to his work. After all, so many tricks of the psychotherapy trade are mere surface decoration for what is really important: unhurried attention, empathy, and genuine concern; the same qualities that have become increasingly hard to find in the U.S. health care system.

Before Enrique and I left the leprosarium, I took a few photos. We shared coffee with Sor Carmen, and I volunteered that I would try to bring medical supplies on another visit. "If only you could return in December," Enrique mused, "you would see things then unlike anything you can even imagine!" The twinkle in his eye was becoming familiar. He described the annual pilgrimage to the Church of San Lázaro, a monumental event that built to crescendo over several days, culminating in a midnight mass on the eve of the 17th of December. Tens of thousands of pilgrims converged on the site from all over Cuba, some by foot, others, on their hands and knees, each seeking divine intervention for an ill loved one or fulfilling a pledge of gratitude for a cure. I put the date on my mental calendar, needing contingency plans in case our research project fell through.

I thanked Sor Carmen and gave her the box of chocolates that the Argentines had spared—big Ohio buckeyes, dollops of peanut butter dipped in dark chocolate. Although my experience with sisters had been limited, I had once shared fudge-covered banana splits with two Maryknoll sisters in Nicaragua. Watching the pair sensually roll the ice cream on their tongues had left a lasting impression, and I anticipated Sor Carmen's response. Her smile broadened and her eyes opened wide at the whiff of chocolate.

Driving home to Vedado, Enrique gunned the engine of his weary car. With his eyes focused on the road ahead, he thought out loud. "During the pilgrimage, the roads to El Rincón are closed to regular traffic. To really see it, you would need to be there a few days ahead of time. Maybe you could stay with the sisters at the convent."

~

Belkis had a late lunch waiting for us, an omelet, *congrí*, fried plantains, and a vegetable salad that she had gone to some effort to make, knowing how I missed greens. As I sat down to eat, I realized that their Great Dane was nowhere to be seen or heard.

"Where is Emilord?" I asked.

Enrique and Belkis exchanged glances in awkward silence. "Old Havana," Enrique replied quietly. "She ate too much and had too many skin problems. The anti-fungal medicine she needed was too expensive and hard to find."

Belkis was relieved to have less commotion in the house. Enrique was sad, but already considering his replacement. "Did you know," he asked, "a Chihuahua can be sustained with the amount of food that fits in a tea cup?"

Our proposal died with a fizzle. We were never told no, but we were never given the go-ahead either. The political mood of MINSAP shifted in a direction that made me hesitant to keep pushing for a definitive response. Between December when we left our final proposal in Dr. Portilla's hands and January when I returned to Cuba for a second month of hopeful waiting, the dengue epidemic had worsened. Hundreds of people had fallen ill and a number had died. How many was unclear; not even Enrique, an epidemiologist, could find out. In a country where prevention was the lauded cornerstone of health care, the outbreak represented a public image calamity for MINSAP. A physician from outside the health ministry had been appointed to oversee efforts to squelch the outbreak, and rumor had it that a major shakeup was brewing.

By the time we abandoned hope for our project, I was without regret, except for the hassle of having to be prepared to deal creatively with the OFAC police in order to continue returning to the country that held me in its grip. I was ready for change. I'd spent enough of my life in the dry realms of scientific rigor. Now I wanted moisture.

"What is a woman like you doing in Cuba?" Gary's question echoed in my head, each time pushing me closer to the truth: neither research nor writing was really the draw. I had come in search of Something Big to pry me out of my velvety rut and hurl me toward richer and loamier soil, soil in which who knew what might grow.

chapter 13

Ariel never mentioned poetry again. Cockroaches appeared but not the promised toilet seat. When a MINSAP exterminator clouded the apartment to the level of toxicity required by the anti-dengue campaign, I discovered that what was politically acceptable in the abstract was offensive in the particular. And with my arm in a sling, I was in no shape to take on household chores. The fantasy that having an apartment of my own in Old Havana would compensate for the one I hadn't claimed for myself in 1969 was short-lived, although acting on adventurous impulse had been its own reward.

So when Ariel announced that he needed to raise the rent yet again, I didn't clamber to stay. I can't remember what his excuse was this time but I thought he'd already been trolling for tourists with deeper pockets, ready to reel them in with one lure or another. Unless I was willing to pay an additional five dollars a day, he said, I needed to find another place to stay.

"I would like to still be friends and help you in any way possible," he added, shamelessly glossing over his bait-and-switch tactics. I thought of the eleven departed Argentines and felt sympathy for them. Then, like them, I decided to leave.

The night before I vacated the apartment, Ariel dropped by to announce that I could stay without a change in rent after all. Apparently a better prospect had failed to materialize. I enjoyed declining his offer, abandoning him to his empty apartment. When I wouldn't change my mind, he looked crestfallen, though I was beyond imagining that his disappointment was more than fiscal. Giving up hope that I would renege, he offered to slice a fresh pineapple for my last breakfast and told me to keep in touch.

My new arrangement was a tribute to Enrique's sound earlier advice: a *casa particular* conveniently located near the Habana Libre Hotel, a block from La Rampa and a five minute walk to his house. Though I was sorry that my foray into independent living had been abruptly truncated, I had to admit that this was a better arrangement. The apartment with my new hosts was roomy in contrast to the match-box quarters of Old Havana. My bedroom was large and comfortable, and my private bath had a seat on the toilet and a shower with plentiful hot water that offered luxurious relief from heat and grime. I shared the apartment with a sixtyish woman named Ibis, her eighty-year-old mother Estella, and two dogs, one Scottie and the other, a grotesquely obese and wildly affectionate Chihuahua named Princesa. The deal was straightforward: a room and breakfast for twenty-five dollars a day. I would have to handle my own laundry. Ibis and Estella were cordial though initially a bit reserved.

Upon seeing my sling and the contusion on my arm, Ibis disappeared into her bedroom to fetch a cache of first aid materials composed of donations from previous lodgers: cotton, gauze, antibiotic ointment, iodine. She insisted on vigorously scrubbing my wound with a rough cloth moistened with alcohol. *"Aguántate un momentico,"* she instructed. Bear this a minute. Then she applied antiseptic. I mentioned that the wound was uncovered because I had never been given a bandage at the clinic. She shook her head and sighed, "We have doctors who are *muy, muy, muy buenos* and many hospitals, but what can they do without resources?" Her mother piped in, "Yes, if you go to the hospitals, there is nothing there." Ibis disappeared again and returned with bandages and adhesive tape to finish the job. Ibis repeated this ritual every day. She prided herself on her medical knowledge, insisting that daily debridement of the wound was the only way I could avoid scarring. I complied, grimacing through her energetic scrubs.

I appreciated their concern for my injury and watched Ibis and her mother soften toward me from one day to the next. Clean laundry magically materialized and Estella even ironed my linen shirt. At first the breakfasts she served me, while shuffling around in a white slip and a red sweater, were Spartan, but then bits of ham and cheese began to appear with the bread and coffee, the addition of protein a positive sign.

Estelle started talking with me in the mornings although her voice was so raspy and her teeth so few that I understood little. I guessed what I thought she might be saying and responded accordingly, relieved that she either failed to realize that I was making it up or never let on that she knew. When Ibis volunteered to lower the price of the room if I returned to their apartment in April, I knew I had won them over.

The SS *Universe*, the sailing vessel of the Semester at Sea program, had just docked in the harbor of Old Havana. Cuba was the first point of call on their spring voyage, offering the opportunity for hundreds of American college students to experience the country for the first time. Having sailed with my husband and daughter on two previous voyages of the ship, I knew the program well. When I heard that they would have a private audience with Fidel Castro, I was determined to use whatever tactics were required to garner an invitation. I wanted to see The Bearded One for myself. The fact that I had no current connection with the ship was an obstacle to be overcome.

At the harbor, passengers streamed off the gangplank into the streets like lemmings off a cliff. I watched one young man hesitate, hovering at the edge of his known world and surveying the beyond of Havana. I wanted to call out, "It's okay. Cuba doesn't bite. Jump in!" but held my breath and watched, as he shifted his weight forward onto the cobblestones without my help. His behavior looked like the enactment of a script hard-wired through human evolution: hesitation, scanning, action. I recognized myself in the sequence. For too many years, I had been stalled in hesitation mode, too tentative and obsessive to take bold action on my own behalf. By risking Cuba, I was falling in love with my life again.

Amidst the crowds, I saw the man I was looking for—the familiar face of one of the administrators. Max recognized me and we raced through a verbal catch-up to the bottom line—would he let me tag along to hear *El*

Comandante? When we parted, I had a ticket in my pocket that identified me as legit.

I arrived at El Palacio de Convenciones as busloads of uniformed young communists unloaded and herded into the building. I merged with the crowd of Cubans and *norteamericanos*, climbed the stairs, and handed over my ticket. In exchange I was offered a ham and cheese sandwich and a soft drink—a Tu Cola, ("*your* cola"), in ironic distinction, I presumed, to the Coca Cola of the Imperialist.

The contemporary amphitheater was full of students, faculty, and staff from the ship. I settled into a comfortable leather chair equipped with a headphone for simultaneous translation. Over the front stage hung a large banner with the photographs of five Cubans who had recently been imprisoned for espionage against the United States. Next to the Cuban Five were images of school children in their Pioneer uniforms and one of a massive political demonstration with thousands of waving red, white, and blue Cuban flags. After several choral pieces and introductions, Fidel Castro entered from the right and walked to the mike at the center of the stage to a welcoming surge of applause. He stood alone in front of two dozen members of his entourage who sat at a long table. *El Comandante* began to speak. It was just after six o'clock.

Seeing Castro on the nightly television news hadn't prepared me for the charm and stature of his physical presence. He was taller than I had imagined. He wore his authority well, standing ramrod straight with heels together, dressed in a green military uniform. He spoke without notes, without a podium, and without a glass of water at his side. He barely moved during the several hours that I watched him. His voice was soft and reminded me of Pablo Neruda reading his poetry.

He asked for a "dialogue" and invited questions. Eager hands flew up. The first question was about the U.S. military base at Guantánamo Bay and its use for holding prisoners from Afghanistan. Fidel Castro's response, delivered in soliloquy, took one hour and forty-five minutes. He began with a detailed history of Cuba from colonial times forward and, master of the tangent, covered the transmission of yellow fever, bits of baseball lore, and the death of Napoleon in his digressions. He eventually meandered back to the question, noting that the existence of the base was granted by the Cuban constitution a century earlier and expressing appreciation to the United States for informing him of what was happening with prisoners. He mentioned that he was willing to assign Cuban doctors to attend to the medical needs of the prisoners at Guantánamo and offered to help fight terrorism in any way possible. With humor and warmth, he referred to several members of the group seated behind him in his monologue, calling one "too skinny" and asking another how old he had been at *el triunfo*.

A second question posed to Castro focused on when he would allow free elections. Another hour passed in lengthy discourse as he expounded on the importance of education, implying that without education, there was no freedom and that the Cuban people were still in the education process. He mentioned José Martí as having written abundant poetry to inspire the Cuban people, quoting him as saying, "Where there is no culture, there is no freedom." He cited social science research on the role of parental education in mediating the effects of divorce on children, and quoted a UNESCO report that showed Cuban school children to be significantly ahead of all other Latin American countries in math and Spanish. He provided no direct answer to the question asked.

I was switching back and forth between English and Spanish on my headset, but my attention was fading in both languages. Several members of his entourage were slumped and sleeping.

El Comandante was still going strong at ten o'clock, when I needed a bathroom and was beginning to think about a pillow and a bed. By this time a number of students and faculty were wandering about taking photographs and some were leaving. Finally, irritated by the presumption that anyone warranted an audience for four hours straight, I snuck out. The next day I would learn that he had continued to speak for another three hours.

I took a taxi and was dropped off across the street from Ibis' flat. Climbing the front steps I glimpsed a young boy out of the corner of my eye who flitted forward, grabbed my cloth satchel, and sprinted off into the shadows. It happened so quickly I didn't have time to be frightened by the little thief. Flustered, I collected myself. He hadn't taken my purse, just a bag with odds and ends in it: a notebook with my notes about the evening, the cloth hat that I wore to keep the sun out of my eyes, two blank computer disks, and a guidebook.

I knocked on the window of the apartment and Ibis and Estelle emerged. Within five minutes four *policía* were crowding me on the front stoop and interrogating me in a friendly and concerned manner as neighbors watched. One officer asked me to describe the boy.

Without thinking, I responded. "Skinny, maybe ten years old," I offered. "He was wearing dark clothes and his skin was the color of *café con leche.*" The officer excused himself to use his radio. Another disappeared and returned a few minutes later with his hand on the collar of a wide-eyed child, looking askance. The scared youngster was coal black.

"Is this him?" the officer asked? "No," I responded immediately. Was this racial profiling? I wanted to ask, but apprehensions about where this might lead tapped me on the shoulder.

To my relief no other suspects appeared. I couldn't finger any child when I knew nothing of what would happen to him as a result. Jails were no place for children. And I hadn't lost much. My notes about Castro were still in my head. The hat could be replaced. And I rarely relied on the guidebook anymore. I chuckled at the thought of the poor boy who, upon examining his stash, would find so little of use.

I had never worried about street crime in Cuba, though I used common sense in keeping my belongings modest and inconspicuous when I was on foot. Police seemed to be on every corner in the well-trafficked part of the city, and ordinary citizens were forbidden to own firearms, thus eliminating what I most feared in cities at home. I never found out who alerted the police to my situation, but the avalanche of officers in response to a petty theft both reinforced my sense of safety and piqued my awareness of omnipresent state surveillance. I imagined the fright of the boy being pursued. I didn't know then how close I would later come to being in his position.

~

On the eve of my departure for home, I felt the undertow of restlessness that inevitably accompanied my geographic transitions. It had been a month chocked-full of new experience. The relationship with Enrique and Belkis had evolved from the formality of *usted* to the *tú* of friendship. I had made a new friend in Gary, and although he had returned to the United States ahead of me, we were already in email contact. Seeing Fidel had been a serendipitous bonus.

And while our research proposal had dead-ended at MINSAP, my adventures in "health research" had taken off. My slip and fall had propitiously catapulted me into the Cuban medical system. I had sampled the medical care available for tourists—solicitous care in a lovely clinic, short on bandages and X-ray film, but cheap—and the emergency room where I would have been treated had I been Cuban, a dilapidated facility crowded with people waiting. Nurse-sisters, doctors, and landladies had shared story after story about suffering caused by embargo-related shortages of drugs, reagents, and medical equipment. I was learning much.

As to my personal quest, I wasn't sure where all this was leading me, but I was becoming increasingly determined that I wouldn't just go back to a windowless office in Ohio. How could I relinquish the rich world I was expanding into and voluntarily return to my cage? Even in a muddle with my arm in a sling, I was feeling more positive about the future than I had in a long time. Thanks to Gary, I was more aware of *having* a future, one that could encompass more than I had previously imagined.

~

No trip to or from Cuba was ever straightforward. I always had to overnight somewhere between the two psychological poles of Havana and Ohio. This time I would fly home via Cancun, staying the night at a hotel on the beach.

Enrique and Belkis insisted on driving me the twenty kilometers from their home to the airport. I welcomed their help, and the day before my departure I slipped Enrique a ten dollar bill for gasoline. Although he received about five gallons a month as part of his government ration, fuel beyond the ration was available only in dollars and his salary was entirely in pesos. As we climbed into the car, I wondered if he had used the bill to buy gas on the black market, perhaps from another physician who had stolen it from the health ministry where he worked. Such practices were commonplace, the source of black market fuel depending on which state ministry one had access to. *Es Cuba,* I thought. *Se inventan.* Cubans invent. Resourcefulness was the national virtue.

My suitcase was heavy with books: the book on Carlos Finlay from the oldest communist in Cuba and three hefty medical texts representing the state of family medicine and public health on the island. Enrique wouldn't let me pay for these. They were his gift, he insisted, *"por la amistad."*

The flight from Havana to Mexico took less than an hour. The road from the Cancun airport to the Solymar Hotel where I had booked a room was wide and smooth, flanked by a glitz of billboards in a rainbow of colors: cigarettes, luxury hotels, a bottle of liquor twelve feet high, and gigantic airbrushed images of women's body parts everywhere—legs, cleavage, sultry eyes. We zoomed by a sign that said "*The Millennial Body,*" but speed prevented me from discerning whether plastic surgery or cosmetics were being sold. I'd become accustomed to the complete absence of commercial culture in Cuba, and as the billboards flipped by like a shuffle of cards I was put off by their vulgarity.

The hotels along the beachfront looked like plastic buildings from a child's game. Stucco walls and designer landscapes obscured even visual access to the beach. I imagined Cuba post-Castro, "opened up" and engulfed by corporate, capitalist, consumer culture. How long would the finest reefs left in the Caribbean survive, should the U.S. have its way with Cuba—Cuba, with thousands of miles of pristine beaches to develop and millions of people to subjugate into roles of hotel maid and bellhop?

By the time I checked in I was hungry. The hotel offered a gourmet Mexican buffet and, after weeks of scrounging for vegetables and variety, I was eager. Spread before me was more food than I had seen in a month. Crowding me at the table were *gringo*s with beer bellies and sunburns. Their shirts were too loud. Eating by myself, I eavesdropped.

"The people here are so nice. They work so hard."

"I should learn Spanish sometime."

"They never finish anything. The things they make just fall apart when you get home."

I looked at the guacamole on my plate. It was the color of Enrique's car. I felt paranoid, as if these strangers were insulting members of my family. Pangs of yearning and anxiety overtook me; I was surfacing too fast out of the depths of Cuba. I needed rescue from this bends, but how?

Another woman sat by herself at a nearby table. She was about my age, and I liked her flowing brightly-flowered dress. Hoping to regain my equilibrium, I willed myself to be social. Yes, she said, she was traveling by herself. She had checked into the hotel for a month on an all-inclusive package—three meals a day, lodging, drinks, and a weekly massage.

Hoping for common ground, I thought of how I would spend a month of leisure in the sun. "Do you read?" I asked.

"No," she replied, dashing my hopes for congenial company.

"And you?" she asked. "What brings you here?"

Could I say that I was a burned out academic who was thinking of jumping out of the Ivory Tower?—a would-be writer who had become enamored with Cuba?

"I'm on my way home," I replied, and looked away.

A young couple, each wearing white Bermuda shorts over pasty legs, waddled up to the buffet and scooped whipped chocolate desserts into parfait glasses.

People spoke English here. It jangled in my ears. After struggling with the opacity of Havana street-Spanish, the transparency of my native tongue made me feel raw and exposed. These tourists—chatting affably with each other, sipping margaritas, and helping themselves to seconds—were my compatriots. They just wanted to escape the late winter doldrums of the North Country, an impulse I should have been able to appreciate. I'd been an escapee too. But I was more than that now, altered by Cuba in ways I didn't yet understand and evolving in directions not yet clear. With all that churned inside me, I couldn't bridge the divide.

part 3

a bigger life

chapter 14

The chunky Chihuahua greeted me with fits of yipping and jumping when I pushed open the door. Ibis and her mother appeared close behind with more civilized hellos, looking more different from each other than I had remembered—elderly Estella tall, pale, and gaunt, her daughter Ibis short, red-headed, and round. The cool air of the apartment was welcome respite after the arduous trip.

For my third month-long stay in Cuba, I decided to wriggle through one of the cracks in the travel ban by claiming eligibility to travel on general license to do professional research. I had no other choice if I wanted to return. With our proposal missing in action and presumed dead, DISARM could no longer justify my travel on their specific license. Since general license is an "assumed" status, there was no official piece of paper granted ahead of time to document legality, but academic cognoscenti had assured me that I should encounter no problem. I booked a direct flight from Miami to Havana, using the charter company that had managed the Cuba to and fro since the seventies.

The old-guard Cuban Americans of Miami considered Fidel Castro the devil incarnate and travelers to Cuba his disciples, presumed guilty of prolonging his dictatorial hold by infusing the country with their dollars. The powers-that-be at Miami International did not take kindly to Cuba travelers.

Every possible obstacle to smooth travel was placed in the path of would-be transgressors of the Miami moral code, even if they were technically "legal."

I arrived at the airport three hours early as advised and discovered that passengers to Cuba were screened separately from all others. Twice I was required to remove my shoes for inspection. Agents scanned me, patted me down, and required me to unload and reassemble my backpack several times.

With each trip to Cuba I accumulated a longer list of items to bring to one person or another. This time I carried two large boxes of gauze, eight bottles of anti-inflammatory medicines, and two-hundred pairs of surgical gloves for the sisters at the leprosarium, and for Enrique, a blood glucose monitor for his use in a research project, a copy of the *New York Times*, and a bottle of premium whisky. For myself, I had packed thirty meal replacement bars to save time that would otherwise be spent foraging for food. At two dollars a pound for surplus weight, additional charges quickly mounted to over forty dollars plus a fifty-dollar departure fee. By the time I was cleared to proceed to the gate, the economic advantage of flying from Miami rather than through a third country had been obliterated.

The Cuban Americans endured the same treatment as they struggled to manage mammoth overloaded bags that garnered even heavier charges. Most were on their way to visit family members and they pushed all limits to carry the maximum load of medicines and consumer goods to needy parents and siblings. The fellow behind me was philosophical about the hassle. "It's Miami!" he shrugged.

The departure gate was at the far end of an empty concourse devoid of other flights. When I finally arrived I plopped down in a seat. To my surprise a trio of officers in Office of Homeland Security uniforms with silver badges was working the crowd. The two men and one woman encircled first one waiting passenger then the next, interrogating each and hovering like vultures over carrion.

They approached the young woman next to me. An agent gruffly asked her when she had last been to Cuba. He sounded accusatory. Who exactly would she be visiting? What was their address? She stammered a nervous response. Apparently, the officers were mandated to enforce the travel restrictions, making sure she had family on the island that she was legally qualified to visit and that she wasn't visiting them more often than the permitted once a year. I winced at the thought of having to go through such an inquisition. The scene struck me as un-American, their uniforms and badges notwithstanding. Wasn't seeing your mother more than once a year encompassed by the right to "life, liberty and the pursuit of happiness?"

My turn was next. The three stood over me. Why was I going to Cuba? This wasn't Gary asking a personal question. This was The Government. I hadn't expected this interrogation and had only moments to prepare. I knew I should project composure and self-confidence. I riffled through my papers and handed the officers my professional card and copies of letters from my university asserting my professional mission. I mentioned an international medical conference I would be attending and paraphrased the criteria for travel on general license: I was a "full time professional in the United States" with a "full-time schedule of research activity in Cuba" with "reasonable possibility of disseminating" what I learned. I prayed that they wouldn't press for details, that my vague reference to "research and writing on health" would suffice.

Luckily it did. To my relief they were at least marginally satisfied with my explanation and moved on to peck at other prey. The woman officer lagged an instant behind, and when the men couldn't see her, she patted me on the shoulder. If I hadn't felt so intimidated, I would have asked her how she felt about the regulations she was required to enforce. Did she go home to children at night and think about divided Cuban-American families?

I boarded and collapsed into my assigned seat, passive and relieved. The pursuit of a one hour flight had become an ordeal. On board was the highest concentration of Cuban American passengers of any flight I had been on. From snatches of conversation I gleaned that several passengers were traveling to Havana for the first time in many years. For others, this coming and going was routine, the only option for maintaining ties within families divided by geography and politics.

With the first sighting of Cuban soil, the planeload erupted in exuberant applause. Old men and women craned their necks to get views of their native land, and mothers pointed out the windows and gestured to their children to look. The plane buzzed with chatter, and I too felt buoyant with anticipation. My Hispanic self flickered on. With no Anglo Americans in sight to remind me of where I was from, I could imagine that I was Cuban, one of the tens of thousands of Cubans and Cuban Americans who have traversed these straits since the *Triunfo de la Revolución*—seeking refuge, reunion, or opportunity. By the time we touched down, my ears had made the transition to Spanish.

~

A smiling curve of papaya accompanied the scrambled eggs and ham that Ibis set before me the next morning. Estella, in her scarlet cardigan, leaned against the stove. How was my arm? she asked—or at least I thought that's what I heard. My ability to understand her toothless mumble hadn't improved. I raised my arm to show her the results of Ibis's curative efforts—smooth skin and no scar. She nodded in approval.

Ibis asked about my family and I realized that I hadn't asked them about theirs since I had arrived, a significant violation of Cuban conversational norms. Worse, I couldn't remember if Ibis had children. I asked.

"No," she responded, her affect flat. "I never had children. When I was young, life was so uncertain. There was the Bay of Pigs, then fears of invasions and bombs from the United States."

She spoke slowly as if listening to herself. "I didn't want a child unless I could be sure that the child would have a better and easier life than mine. The dangerous times never ended, but my time to have children did." She paused. "Even now there are such sophisticated weapons. Who knows what might happen?" She drew her hand across her throat with a grunt.

After breakfast I finished unpacking, putting to one side the gifts and supplies destined for Enrique or the convent. In spite of exceeding the weight limits, I had packed light when it came to personal belongings. I took pleasure in the simplicity of stuff that my life in Cuba required. Two thousand square feet of living space full of "necessities" at home were pared down to the truly essential in my suitcase—good shoes, summer clothes, toiletries, earplugs—about three cubic feet of tightly compacted supplies. I enjoyed the ritual of settling in: stacking the clothes in the wooden armoire, arranging my toiletries on the bathroom shelves, finding a safe corner for my laptop. I stashed my money belt full of dollars in the freezer of the refrigerator in my room. The chill felt good the next day when I slipped the belt on under the waistband of my skirt and crossed the steamy diesel-fumed streets between my lodging and the medical conference at the Hotel Nacional.

chapter 15

The teenager had a sprinkle of acne on her cheeks. "What can I do about my blemishes?" she asked her doctor, looking up at him expectantly from under her brown bob. "Don't pick them!" the handsome young physician admonished. "And make sure you keep your hands clean. Can you show me how you should wash your hands?" I could hardly believe my ears—a doctor asking a near-adult to demonstrate hand-washing, but she didn't hesitate. Obediently, she walked to the small sink in the corner of the consulting room, took a sliver of soap, scrubbed her hands vigorously under running water, and held them high in the air for her doctor to see—fronts and backs. "Good!" he responded, grinning and nodding his approval.

He was cute. With his crooked front tooth and dark brown eyes, the doctor projected a mischievous and boyish air. From my seat in a corner of his office, I enjoyed the undercurrent of flirtation between them. She must find him attractive, I thought. I did.

We were in Cerro, one of the oldest and poorest municipalities of Havana. I was there at the doctor's invitation. Like a row of dominoes the right circumstances had fallen into place, and I'd been offered a front row seat in the theater of Cuban family medicine. I was elated. I had exchanged predictable and frustrating MINSAP visits for the pleasures of this unsanctioned version of research.

~

I had met Félix at an international medical conference at the Hotel Nacional where he spoke at a symposium about his role with a Cuban medical mission sent to El Salvador to help the local population combat a year-long epidemic of dengue fever. He described walking door-to-door in a war zone, persuading people on both sides of the political conflict about the importance of mosquito control. Health, not politics, was his priority, and person-to-person education the means to achieve it. His charm and sparkling intellect drew me into his orbit, and when he shared that he was now a family physician in Cerro, I dared hope he might give me a chance to visit his practice.

"*¿Por qué no?*" he replied, when I asked, flashing me a smile. Soon he was giving me directions to his *consultorio.* I was to meet him there the following Tuesday. He would be seeing patients in the clinic in the morning and making home visits in the afternoon, and I could accompany him for the day.

Since my twenties, I have harbored a secret identity as a medical voyeur. I like watching what doctors do: how they merge the semi-science of diagnosis with the art of relating to their patients or sacrifice one aspect for the other; how they project what they know and hide their insecurities in deep cover; how they sometimes, in spite of themselves, act compassionately and endearingly human, transparent through their white coats. The family medicine scene in the United States had become so routine to me that it no longer compelled my interest, but the Cuban version was a different matter. I was thrilled at Félix's invitation.

I spent the weekend in eager anticipation, cramming medical Spanish and reviewing what I knew about primary health care in Cuba. Family doctors were at the heart of the system, accessible to all, living among their patients, each physician responsible for a clearly defined population of families. Doctor-nurse teams worked proactively to identify and address risks to the health of those in their jurisdiction. As Félix would put it, "We are responsible, not for health care *in* the community, but for the health *of* the community."

Early Tuesday, I gave a *taxista* the address of Felix's *consultorio.* We entered his old neighborhood on Calzada de Cerro, a broad street lined with adjoining worn-out houses strung together with front porticos and rows of columns that looked like old teeth that had long ago lost their enamel. The boulevard gave way to side streets and then a small park where old people in a *Círculo de Abuelos* were gathering under the trees for their morning calisthenics. From the corner of the park, we climbed a short hill, and I was dropped in front of a white two-story building. I stepped onto the curb and faced a formidable cement staircase that led up to Félix's clinic and his apartment. Accessibility for the handicapped was clearly low priority.

I paused at the top of the climb to take in the view. Looking across the urban landscape toward the Plaza of the Revolution, I could see the monument to José Martí, leader of the Cuban independence movement against Spain. Later, Félix would tell me, "Fidel made real the dreams of Martí. It was Martí who said that the best medicine was not that which cures but that which prevents."

Félix greeted me with a kiss on the cheek. He was wearing jeans, polished black shoes, and a crisp white *guayabera* shirt that set off his golden skin. He oriented me briefly to his situation and his community. He had lived and worked in Cerro since 1994. It was his first professional post, one that he had assumed after graduating from medical school at the University of Havana and completing two years of required social service in the far eastern part of the country.

Cerro was not a popular post for physicians. The neighborhood was dense with colonial buildings, and as a result, its residents suffered from the humidity, poor ventilation, and social problems that went with deteriorating housing. Children frequently had asthma. Older patients with heart and pulmonary conditions suffered. Family conflicts were exacerbated by crowding. These realities presented challenges to the health care team responsible for the well-being of the community. "If we had class in Cuba—which we don't," he explained, "Cerro would be considered low class."

Buzzing interrupted our conversation. The noise, remarkably similar to the sound of a mosquito in one's ear, was fumigation equipment in use.

MINSAP had sent exterminators and social workers to partner with the staff of neighborhood *consultorios* in community education and mosquito eradication efforts.

We descended the flight of stairs that separated Félix's apartment from the *consultorio* below, and entered through a sparsely furnished waiting room with hard wooden chairs. On the wall, a poster summarized information on the two-hundred families served by this clinic, including the numbers of patients in each of four categories (healthy, at risk, acutely or chronically ill, and disabled) and the types of illnesses that affected the community. I paused to read. Cancer and cardiac disease were the leading causes of death, just as in the United States and other developed countries. Only forty percent of houses were judged to be structurally sound. Seven percent of the population was estimated to have difficulty meeting basic needs for food, shelter, recreation, or companionship. Looking over my shoulder as I read, Félix commented that these data were from an analysis of community health that he was required to conduct each year. Few family doctors at home could speak so knowledgeably about the communities in which they practiced.

A short hallway connected the waiting room to two consulting rooms and a tiny rest room. "When you need a bathroom, go to my apartment," Félix said as we passed by. "This one no longer works." We entered the room where he saw patients. It was about twelve feet square, with a simple desk and chair, an examining table, and fluorescent ceiling lights. A few books sat on a small file cabinet. Two posters, gifts from the community, adorned the wall; one exhorting the viewer to save the ozone layer, the other, a hotel travel poster. A third poster showed a mother cuddling her newborn under the words *"piel a piel,"* recommending skin to skin contact for babies.

His nurse had a desk in the next room where medical charts were kept. There, decorating one wall was a hand-illustrated poster about four feet long, neatly framed and featuring mothers looking tenderly at their nursing babies, and twenty-five reasons to breast-feed. "It was a group effort," Félix said. "I made the wooden frame myself." He pointed to the image of a dark-skinned man holding a baby, "I made sure there was a photograph that showed the role of fathers—with a man who looked like he could be from here."

From nine o'clock until one-thirty, I sat quietly in the corner of the consulting room while Félix tended a steady stream of patients. He introduced me briefly to each, announcing that I was a visitor from a medical school in the United States. My presence was met with no resistance. His patients were mostly women with garden-variety complaints—garden-variety for a developed country, that is. No childhood diarrhea, no major infectious diseases, no parasitic infestations, no malnutrition—the problems familiar to me from my Peace Corps days and typical of impoverished communities in Latin America. The mix of presenting complaints was remarkably similar to what brought people to the family medicine clinic where I worked at home—minor illnesses, follow-ups on tests, the "worried well."

A young man needed an employment physical for his new job as a lifeguard. "For that kind of work, I'll need to screen you for sexually transmitted diseases," Félix explained. "You know it's best to have just one regular partner. Otherwise you need to use protection. And you will need to be careful," he went on, grinning. "Girls pretend to drown and then want you to give mouth-to-mouth." The young man smiled sheepishly and averted his eyes.

A middle-aged woman had just discovered she was pregnant and wanted an abortion, her fourth. Félix referred her to a hospital where she could stay overnight and receive a first-trimester suction abortion. He reminded her that using condoms could have prevented the pregnancy. From the flatness in his voice, I knew this discussion had occurred before. The woman sighed and looked my way, as if there were some things that only another woman could understand. "*No es fácil,*" she remarked.

After she departed, Félix commented that he didn't like abortion and preferred to work on prevention. "But there were many problems—even deaths—from illegal abortion before the revolution, and at least she will get a safe one."

Between patients Félix let me look through medical charts. I was puzzled by a slip of paper requesting a laboratory test with "N/R" written next to the order. "*No hay reactivos,*" Félix explained. The reagents necessary to perform the tests were not available. It was the same story I had heard at the leprosarium. I checked other charts. All were peppered with the N/R notation. Because of these shortages, Félix explained, tests for kidney function or blood glucose were often not possible. He often had to rely on clinical examination and judgment alone to gauge whether a hypertensive patient was having kidney damage or a diabetic was in good control of her diet.

According to my new colleague, tests that couldn't be done and medicines that weren't available sometimes led to devastating results: "Over the years, more Cubans have died from *el bloqueo* than all the people who died in 9/11." From his gentle tone it was clear that his blame was directed at my government and not at me. Even so, I couldn't suppress a sense of shame, as if I were at fault.

The next patient was a plump and pretty teenager complaining of a headache, joint aches, and a painful belly. As she began to speak, the nurse interrupted with a knock on the door. "The fumigators want to spray your apartment. Is that okay?" she asked Félix. He tossed her his house key and refocused his attention on his patient. He did a physical, ordered sinus films and a pelvic ultrasound, and talked to her about the likelihood that she had premenstrual syndrome. Sinusitis was another possibility. Did she smoke or was anyone at home smoking? "If your father is smoking, we'll have to start a campaign to get him to stop," he said. She would need to come back after the tests were complete. As she went to leave, she kissed him on the cheek.

A woman in her fifties entered the room next, carrying an X-ray that had been taken the day before at the polyclinic that provided diagnostic services and specialty care to this and a dozen other *consultorios.* Félix held the film up to the light-box and told her that her arm pain was the result of degenerative changes in the cervical spine. Physical therapy and traction might help, but that the problem would probably be chronic. "X-ray film is always in short supply," he said, turning in my direction. "Lately, only small film plates have been available. You can imagine the kind of difficulties that creates with large patients or complex problems." I hardly needed to be reminded.

"Resolve and invent are the verbs we use most!" he said. The shrug of his shoulders and his hands in the air framed his easy smile.

The last patient was a pretty young woman with mild chest pain. Teasing her, Félix commented that she had been a very difficult teenager. She laughed. "Yes, but I was saved by a special program," she said. The program served people between 18 and 30 who were neither working nor in school. It was the inspiration of *El Comandante* and had been developed by the Organization of Young Communists. She invited me to attend a meeting, then turned back to her doctor and handed him an EKG strip from a test that had been administered at the polyclinic. She noticed a bug on Félix's arm and casually brushed it off.

Félix examined her, reassured her that her heart was fine, and suggested that the problem was muscular, maybe aggravated by stress. She should do more aerobic exercise, take an anti-inflammatory, and rub Chinese pomade on her chest where it hurts. She would be able to find both the anti-inflammatory and the pomade at the local pharmacy where "green medicines" were dispensed along with manufactured pharmaceuticals.

The morning passed quickly. Félix had seen half a dozen patients, spending about twenty minutes with each. He typically saw nine to twelve patients in a morning, but my presence had slowed him down. I concluded that his patients probably saw him for about the same length of time that patients in the United States saw their doctors. Based on what I had observed, however, I thought the quality of interaction contrasted favorably with what I had observed at home. None of Félix's patients were strangers to him. He was distracted by me, but not by insurance or billing forms or excessive paperwork. While deprived of laboratory resources, his clinical judgment had been honed by the necessity of addressing patients' concerns, whether or not there were adequate chemical reagents or X-ray film. I thought of all the doctors I had observed over the years, many harried by the bureaucratic weight of their responsibilities, pushed by medical school debts and managed care companies to labor well beyond the point of satisfaction. I couldn't remember one that had looked as happy in his work as Félix.

We were famished. Félix suggested that we eat at his usual spot, the shoe factory down the street. We walked a block or so and entered what from the street looked like a house. Inside we passed through a front room where a half a dozen workers tapped foot treadles of old sewing machines amid heaping piles of white leather scraps. We exited onto a side patio where we sat on plastic chairs. An old woman scooped yellow rice with tiny bits of unrecognizable meat onto aluminum plates next to thin slices of watery tomato. We drank water from tin cups. It was one of the poorest meals I had been served in Cuba but I ate hungrily, trying not to think about where the meat originated.

Félix seemed self-conscious about the food. "Sometimes there is more when I get here earlier," he said. "We are a country of shared poverty—but not misery." Even as a doctor, Félix shared the poverty of Cuba. Like his patients he depended on the ration book for state-subsidized food. He didn't own a car. Although the state provided him with a modest furnished apartment, the rewards of his work were largely non-material. His salary gave him no more than a slight economic edge.

I thought about lunches I had shared with family doctors at home, lunches personally delivered by curvaceous nubile women in trim dark suits with long polished fingernails, drug company representatives eager to treat physicians to a good meal in exchange for the opportunity to pitch them new pharmaceuticals. "No cookie, no lookie," one of my medical colleagues had once said to a drug rep, so accustomed to being fed that he wouldn't review her informational brochures without culinary incentive. The pharmaceutical flirtation was always fueled by free food and drug samples. The meals provided were generous and predictably fattening; barbecued ribs would preface a talk about the latest anti-cholesterol wonder. The leftovers were usually sufficient to feed the office staff a second day, assuring a warm reception for the representative when she next came to call.

Our forks clinked musically against our aluminum plates. The ineffable experience of being with this good doctor, watching him work, and listening to his stories held me rapt.

chapter 16

After lunch, we returned to the *consultorio* where Félix pulled cards from a file box and organized them to correspond with our afternoon schedule of home visits. Each *tarjeta* represented a household and was preprinted with prompts to facilitate tracking visits. While the frequency of contact depended on the health of family members, either Félix or his nurse visited each house served by their practice at least once a year. "Home visits are the best way to know what people need as opposed to what they ask us for."

With a handful of *tarjetas* in his shirt pocket, Félix led me out of the *consultorio.* I veered toward the narrow sidewalk. "No, better the street," he said, pulling me by my elbow. "In Cerro people still walk down the middle as they did before cars." We claimed the street, and the occasional car accommodated us.

Félix knocked on the door of a modest stucco house where we were greeted by an attractive older woman with salt-and-pepper hair. She waved us inside, unruffled by the unexpected visit of her doctor with a *norteamericana* in tow. A barking mongrel scurried underfoot. Her twelve-year-old grandson Julio was playing a game quietly at a table covered with a red plastic cloth. The boy's father had been a *balsero*, one of hundreds of men and women who had left for the United States in makeshift rafts in the early nineties. The grandmother said that the boy had been asking about his father. She worried that his absence was damaging to the boy. I wondered where the boy's mother was but refrained from asking. Félix reassured Julio's grandmother that what was important was the love in the family. Turning to Julio, Félix suggested that he write a letter to his father. He asked to see the boy's school workbook, perused it, and passed it to me. I opened the notebook to a page where Julio had written, "When I grow up I will be an athlete so that I can travel to other countries with the gold medal."

The grandfather, who had been busy in another room, poked his head in and offered the doctor a cigarette. Félix scowled. "How could I smoke and then advise you not to?" he admonished. "That cigarette has a price!" Félix made a notation on a *tajeta* and shifted his attention back to the grandmother. She had been very healthy.

He touched her lightly on the shoulder and looked at me. "She doesn't *abuse* the clinic. She doesn't *use* it!" he said, chiding her. He pulled a blood pressure cuff out of his bag and wrapped it around her arm. The reading was higher than on previous visits, now borderline hypertensive at 140/90. He encouraged her to exercise more. Perhaps she could join other older people from her neighborhood at the *Círculo de Abuelos* that met each morning in the park. He suggested that she trim her use of salt and follow-up at the *consultorio* for blood pressure checks. Then he turned to her husband, still standing in the doorway.

"If you have to smoke," he said sternly, "go up on the roof so that you at least protect your wife and grandson. We are all breathing your last cigarette right now."

The man looked contrite, but even in the wake of this confrontation, the visit ended cordially with the couple thanking the doctor for the visit.

Fumigation equipment buzzed in the distance as we returned to the street. At almost every doorway someone greeted the doctor, even small children addressing him as Félix. We had walked less than a block when an elderly man in a doorway called to us. He waved us into his house and gestured toward a freezer in his living room. Before we knew it, we were licking homemade peach popsicles with him and his wife. The cool melt was refreshing.

Our next visit was to a housebound diabetic man recovering from the recent amputation of his right leg. His elderly mother led us to his bedroom. He peeked out from under the covers of his bed, unkempt with greasy black hair, looking much older than his forty-five years. He had been a smoker and a drinker, although he had relinquished both vices in the face of his advancing disease. Medicine bottles mingled with framed photographs on his bedside table. He responded to the doctor's queries on his progress and then paused.

"I have something I want to show you," he said, and I realized he was talking to me. He rose from his bed, bare-chested and wearing tan shorts, and hopped awkwardly to the dresser. He opened a drawer and removed a folded plastic bag from which he produced a translucent shard.

"It's a piece of my leg!" he explained proudly. He handed it to me as if it were a communion wafer. I fingered the sacred object and nodded appreciatively.

This was a first, I thought, enjoying the moment. Always, as a psychologist, it was the surprises that gave me the most kick—the perverse pleasure of glimpsing human behavior in the extreme. I handed the bone back to him and he put it away and hopped back to his bed. I suppressed the urge to comment on the universal need to stay connected to one's body parts.

Félix reviewed his patient's medicines and diet along with the post-amputation exercises that had been prescribed at the hospital. The doctor asked how much the operation had cost, and the patient looked startled, until he realized that the question was for my benefit. "*Nada,*" he replied, although he would have to pay the equivalent of two dollars for the prosthetic leg he was waiting for.

A frail, elderly couple was our next stop. They invited us into a small dingy *sala* with just enough chairs to accommodate the four of us. I found it hard to fathom that at every home where we stopped we were welcomed and invited in, even though no one had been warned that the physician would be dropping by. The woman was hypertensive and had recently been treated for giardia, a water-born protozoan parasite. Félix had diagnosed seven cases in the past year. The prevalence of giardia was the result of *el bloqueo* he explained, because of shortages of chemicals for water treatment and materials for plumbing repair. On this visit she complained that she hadn't been sleeping well, and the doctor suggested that she get more exercise.

Considering her reclusive nature, he advised, "If you don't want to join the *Círculo de Abuelos*, you could at least watch them through your front window and exercise along."

The woman's husband suffered from bad lungs and circulation problems caused by smoking and heart disease. He wanted Félix to know that he had cut back on his smoking and was now able to walk a block without getting winded. On his doctor's recommendation, he had started taking *Policosanol*, an anti-cholesterol drug Cubans had developed from sugar cane.

"It is a highly effective medicine—and very popular," Félix remarked with a half wink in my direction. "It has Viagra-like side effects." I had never heard of the drug, unavailable in the United States because of the trade restrictions.

The last visit of the afternoon was to check on a family that had recently weathered a marital crisis. The man of the house had threatened to leave his wife and young children. Although he wasn't home when we dropped by, his wife reported that things had been much better since he had gone to see the psychiatrist at the polyclinic as Félix had recommended. We lingered, sitting comfortably in her *sala*. Félix and the woman discussed her family problems. I was tired from the afternoon of visits and from conversing in Spanish all day without a break. Listening to them I was relieved that the doctor, not I, bore the responsibility of providing help.

"I'll stop by another time to talk with your husband," Félix said as we departed. Once out of the earshot of his patients, he shook his head and sighed. "*¡El médico familiar está en todo!*" The family doctor is involved in everything. From fumigation to family therapy, I thought. The scope of practice for family physicians in the United States was broad too—my colleagues at home dealt with everything from appendicitis to alcoholism to acne. But in the United States, the vast majority practiced only in clinical and hospital settings. So much of the work of prevention and early intervention that Félix had packed into the day had emerged organically by relating to his patients in their homes.

We strolled wearily back to the *consultorio*. At a corner we encountered a slender fellow shouldering a fumigation sprayer and wearing a red government-issue "Special Detachment" T-shirt. He was accompanied by the nurse who worked with Félix. The pair had spent the afternoon going house to house encouraging families to eliminate standing water and allow the exterminator to spray.

As we neared our destination, a young mother sitting in a doorway called out to the doctor. He responded warmly, saying to me, "This is the family that takes care of *me*. They let me use their telephone, since I don't have one." From the interior of the house, a small child appeared. The mother introduced me to her, plump and precocious, now peeking out from behind her mother's legs. "Listen!" the woman said. "She can already say *Aedes aegypti*!" The mother's gentle prompts elicited a tentative *"aaeeday aiipteee"* from the shy little girl. It was the Latin name for the mosquito that transmitted dengue.

It was close to six o'clock when Félix and I reached his apartment. His wife Aidelís, a quiet and pretty nurse, had just arrived home from her post at another *consultorio*. The day's work was not over for either of them. After I said goodbye, she would cook dinner while Félix and a medical resident went to a meeting with community members to plan a neighborhood health fair. The meeting would last an hour, and then he would invite the resident to eat supper at his house while they talked shop. Around nine-o'clock a distressed mother would bring a septic child to his home for examination, and he would arrange for his hospitalization. It would be after ten before Félix and Aidelís had time to relax together.

~

After spending time with Félix, I needed a reality check; I needed to talk with Enrique. Félix seemed almost too good to be true. He knew every person in his neighborhood by name. He cheerfully provided care from dawn to dusk and beyond. He was steeped in idealistic socialist perspective. Could what I had observed possibly be typical of what Cubans experience with their family doctors?

Maybe not. I asked Enrique how things were with his family physician, and he responded, "The doctor assigned to our neighborhood has never visited my family. She wouldn't know me if we bumped into each other on the street!"

He continued. "Some doctors are never at home. They don't want to see any more patients than they have to. They are overwhelmed by their patients' needs and they don't have the option of leaving their careers so they just aren't there." He looked at me directly and repeated for emphasis, "*¡No están!*" His manner was intense. Lest I think I was getting a handle on the complexity around me, he threw more contradictions into the mix. "Some doctors never wanted to go into medicine in the first place. Others want to become specialists but can't," he continued. "The government sets priorities on what is needed and allots places accordingly. Many young people who might have chosen other careers have been obligated to go into family medicine."

He gestured toward Belkis as she emerged from the kitchen with cups of coffee on a tray. "When she was at the university, she was required to train in food chemistry, specializing in meats. Imagine, specializing in meats in a country that hardly has any!" I could feel the simmer of anger in his voice, but when Belkis piped in brightly, the mood shifted. "I was never interested in meat chemistry. We used to do things in our labs like measuring the PH of bread. Afterwards, we ate the samples!"

I thought back to where Félix and I had met—at an international medical meeting at the prestigious Hotel Nacional. Physicians from all over Latin America had attended, but although Cuba had more doctors per capita than any country in the hemisphere and the conference was in their country, few Cubans had participated. I wondered out loud and Enrique explained: "You have to get special permission." He left it to me to read between the lines.

~

I returned to Cerro with a stash of vitamins and analgesics from home that I wanted to leave with Félix for use in his *consultorio.* As I handed him the bottles, he examined each, placing them one by one in the metal cabinet where he kept supplies for his patients. When he saw the large bottle of B vitamins, his face lit up. He held the container high and exclaimed, "This bottle is for *me*!" An air of seriousness passed over his features as he decided whether or not to say more. He sighed. "You see, Juanita, I too have been affected by the blockade. Soon I will tell you." We finished putting the rest of the bottles in the cabinet then climbed the stairs to his apartment where he shared a photo album and his story.

When the Soviet Union collapsed, Félix was completing his internship in the eastern mountains between Santiago de Cuba and Holguín provinces.

There he provided medical care on horseback to a dispersed rural community of two hundred people. The abrupt termination of subsidies and trade from their Russian partner ushered in what Fidel called *el período especial*, the "special period," a time of severe food shortages and economic hardship, unmitigated by any humanitarian aid from the United States.

Coffee was the only cash crop in the region, and Félix and the people he served were dependent on government rations for food. When the food shortages hit his community hard, Félix and his patients resorted to eating wild herbs to subdue their hunger. Over several months, he became thinner and thinner and began to experience strange sensations and numbness in his arms and legs. But that was not the worst of it. One morning, he realized that he could not see his horse although he knew that the animal was tied close by. Wherever he looked was blurry, with clearer patches only at the edges of his vision. He was losing his sight.

Frightened, he finally left his community to seek medical attention in Havana. He was diagnosed as suffering from severe shortages of vitamin B. With improved nutrition and supplemental vitamins, his visual problems resolved, but the peripheral neuropathies remained. Sometimes, he said, when he walked the streets of Cerro to visit his patients, he had to ignore tingling and cramps in his legs.

Félix was one of thousands of Cubans who suffered—and who continued to suffer—from neuropathies induced by the food shortages of the "special period," but he expressed no bitterness as he reminisced over photographs from his years of social service. The pictures showed a young man, gaunt and pale, but happy. "There was one week when I didn't even have shoes," he laughed. He flipped to a picture that featured his younger self, sitting barefoot at a small table and leaning attentively toward a patient. Then he closed the photo album and leaned back, suddenly pensive. "All physicians should have to serve in the countryside," he said. "Medical school taught me about medicine, but the mountains taught me about community."

chapter 17

Without complaint, Phil weathered two harsh winter months alone while I was adventuring in Havana warmth. Each time I returned to Ohio, I would fill our kitchen with stories and he could see that Cuba had rejuvenated my ailing spirits. Although we shared years together in Nicaragua, unlike me, he didn't think that he had been Hispanic in another life. But he did like to travel and he became progressively more curious about the country that was stealing my affections.

Phil is a man who follows the rules, even the ones he might not agree with, so when he decided to visit Cuba during my third stay, he wouldn't consider just hopping a plane in Toronto and visiting illegally, as over a hundred thousand United States citizens do each year. Instead, he enrolled in an educational tour sponsored by Global Exchange that promised to teach him about solar energy developments on the island. It was a perfect match for his interests as a high school physics teacher, and the dates fortuitously coincided with his spring vacation. He was doubly lucky since such people-to-people educational exchanges with Cuba would be eliminated by the U.S. State Department less than two years later.

Our plan was for him to join me during the last week of my March stay. I would travel with his group to Pinar del Rio where they would attend a solar energy conference while I would contrive an itinerary in the health arena. My time with Félix had emboldened me, and free-wheeling my sabbatical journey had become its own adventure, though nerve-wracking at times. I always felt the presence of OFAC, the enforcers of the travel restrictions, at my shoulder. As if a police car were flashing lights in my rear view mirror, I felt anxious no matter what my speed.

~

As you look at a map of Cuba, Pinar del Rio is on the left, about two hundred kilometers southwest of Havana. Cigar aficionados know it is as the capital of the province that produces the finest tobacco and the finest *puros* in the world. An ornate print on a cigar-box seal that I purchased in Old Havana depicts the verdant leafy fields, red dirt, and *guajiros* in straw hats bending over the aromatic plants.

Walking in a town of only a hundred and twenty-five thousand and inhaling country air felt delightful after the soot of Havana. The center of Pinar was a web of confusing, narrow streets that dated back to the 1600s, lined with dozens of one-story cottages strung together like railroad cars. Lean horses pulled wagons of passengers squeezed together on wooden benches. Bike taxis flitted by, pedaled by young boys calling out for fares. Here was a makeshift beauty station where you could sit in the street and have your nails painted. Over there was an outdoor food stand where busy cooks hawked tomato and cheese pizzas.

Nearby, two men were fixing spectacles at a small table inside a storefront. I was carrying Phil's glasses in my pocket. An earpiece had broken while he was in transit, and I volunteered to get it repaired while he was off with his group. I handed the glasses to a gentleman who soldered together the earpiece and handed them back to me. There wasn't a trace of seam where they had been mended.

"¿Cuánto cuesta?" I asked.

"Nada," he replied agreeably, but he didn't decline the dollar I handed him.

Our accommodations the night before had shared none of the appeal of the streets. In a windowless room at a Russian-built hotel we had been repeatedly roused by salsa music booming from the poolside disco. We woke up cranky, and when Phil left to join his group, I set out to find more tranquil accommodations. Although the room was included in his tour package, I had been required to pay an extra twenty dollars a day to stay with him. Surely for that price, I thought, we could both stay in a more pleasant *casa particular.*

I turned down a street adjacent to the hotel that led into a quiet neighborhood. Pausing at a *Círculo de Niños*, a state day care center, I watched children playing in a fenced-in yard. Two boys took turns playing doctor. One jumped onto an imaginary sick bed and lay down. The other listened to his playmate's heart with a plastic stethoscope. Further on, a chorus of twittering and chirps coming from a tiny house on a corner caught my attention. A man in a ragged T-shirt was sitting on a wooden chair in the open doorway.

"¿Suyos?" I inquired, gesturing in the direction of the bird sounds.

"Sí," he responded with obvious pride. *"¿Quiere verlos?"* Would you like to see them?

This *paseo* was already lifting my spirits, and I detoured from my self-appointed task to follow him through the entryway to a room filled with floor-to-ceiling cages, birds in every one. He pushed seeds into one of the cages with his fingers. Most of his birds were native to Cuba, although several had been purchased from abroad.

"Son muy bonitos," I offered, wishing that my Spanish could sustain a more nuanced conversation about birds. Before parting, I asked if he knew anyone in his neighborhood with a room for rent. He pointed to a nearby *casa particular* where macramé planters hanging under the eaves next to a stained-glass window brought bell bottoms and flower children to mind. In the front patio, a large green and yellow cactus dwarfed other plants and flowers. On the wooden door was the triangular sticker that marked this as a home licensed to rent rooms. After my Havana exploits, this looked pretty tame.

A knock brought the *señora* to the door, a stout woman with silvery auburn hair. She introduced herself as Cheche and said that for twenty dollars a night we could have a private room and bath. She was pleased at the prospect of guests, volunteering that it had been difficult for her and her husband to keep their accommodations full since the drop in tourism after the destruction of *"las torres gemelas"* on 9/11.

We moved in later that day. Cheche chatted readily and was quick to serve us icy fruit concoctions each time we returned from outside wilted by the heat. After several getting-to-know-you talks about our families and travel, I mentioned my interest in health care and the effects of the embargo. Over lemonade she responded to my curiosity with her story.

For some time, Cheche had suffered from chronic pain in her shoulders and back and shooting pains down her legs. Recently she had traveled to Havana for a diagnostic workup at a top orthopedic hospital. After a detailed examination and tests, the doctor told her that she had bursitis in her shoulders and compressed vertebrae that were causing nerve impingement and the pains in her back and legs. He prescribed vitamins, an anti-inflammatory called Indocin, a muscle relaxant called meprobamate, and a special corset to support her spine. "When I arrived at the pharmacy, there were no vitamins. There was no Indocin. There was no meprobamate. And I was told there wasn't any material in the country to make the corset!" She threw her hands in the air, exasperated. "I had all the expenses of the trip to Havana and I still have to live with pain!"

Whomever and wherever I asked, Cubans described their medical system in similar terms. It was comprehensive and available to all, and their doctors were compassionate and well-trained. But when people spoke of medicines, their enthusiasm evaporated, and they lamented serious shortages and erratic availability of what they and their family members needed.

Enrique had told me about an enclave of families in the province of Pinar del Rio for whom such shortages presented no problem; they eschewed the use of medicines, instead relying solely on the healing power of water. These *acuáticos* were the remnants of a cult that began in the 1930s around the purported powers of a *curandera* named Antoñica Izquerdo who claimed to have cured her lame son with her ministrations and water from the local springs. His miraculous recovery and her powers as a healer received generous attention from the newspapers of the day, generating a frenzy of interest. Pilgrims from all over Cuba and abroad converged to confer with Antoñica and sample the waters. Sadly, her career came to an abrupt end when she was taken to a lunatic asylum in Havana where she later died. Her legacy was a group of families still devoted to water cures and living in the hills of the Viñales Valley, less than an hour's drive from where I was staying in Pinar del Rio.

Cheche's friend Silvio, a jovial fellow with a paunch and a butch haircut who hung around the house and shared meals, was informed of my interest and offered to take me to meet them. Given chronic food shortages I surmised that sharing food was to share *confianza*, the trust and intimacy of family relation. Banking on the transitive nature of trust, I hired him. We discussed plans. For twenty dollars he would drive me to a farm where I would meet his friend Orlando who would guide me on horseback into the hills where the *acuáticos* lived. The trip would consume the day and I would eat with a family in their home before returning.

The evening before our trip, my thoughts were a mix of excited anticipation and memories of my youthful days in the Peace Corps. On a volcanic island in Lake Nicaragua I had commuted to remote villages on horseback to visit women and children in grass houses and talk with them about their health and nutrition. Although my Spanish had been rudimentary and my behavior must have appeared odd in ways I couldn't even imagine, the *campesino* families had embraced me. Returning home at sunset, I would canter along the beach, passing men pulling in their fishing lines and women folding their laundry bleached and dried by the afternoon sun. Trees adorned with green parrots silhouetted against red sky and the omnipresent breast of the volcano. Now, thirty years later, my dreams were infused with images of Nicaraguan mothers cradling babies, coffee toasting in clay pots, and laughter shared across boundaries of language. My middle-aged persona dissolved during the night and by morning, waiting for my guide, I imagined myself to be young Margaret Mead on horseback.

Silvio pulled up in a shiny green Lada, relaxed and talkative. Old cars being a perennial topic of conversation, I asked him about his. He beamed, pleased to be asked. Against all odds, his Lada had been propelled over four hundred thousand miles on four successive engines, only lately serving as a word-of-mouth taxi.

We wound our way out of town and through low hills and partially cultivated farmland where stands of palm trees punctuated stretches of scrub vegetation. A half-hour passed. As we approached our destination, green protrusions, shaped like the rounded ends of French bread, jutted skyward from the flat valley floor. These were *mogotes,* the distinctive karst formations for which the region was known, first cousins of the mountains depicted in paintings of southern China.

We pulled up in front of a small homestead nestled between a huge *mogote* and a pond. An A-frame tobacco barn covered with grey palm fronds was reflected in the placid waters. A skinny young man with a thin brown mustache emerged from the farmhouse and greeted us, casually handing Silvio an armload of yucca *"para tu familia."* It was Orlando, my guide. He sketched with his hand the route we would take around the mountain behind us and beyond. His services and the use of the horse would cost twenty dollars.

Silvio departed leaving me in his friend's care. He would retrieve me at the end of the day. I looked at my horse, lean as Orlando, and felt an all too familiar surge of wishing that I were slim. He led the horse to a low spot next to a bench. As I mounted, I could feel Orlando on the other side, exerting the full weight of his fragile frame to keep the saddle in place.

Although it had been several years since I had straddled a horse, my feet found the stirrups easily. I had taken lessons as a child but my riding had always been marked more by enthusiasm than skill. I'd only been thrown once but several close calls had taught me the value of caution. All the same, I could barely contain the urge to get moving. I was ready to loosen the reins.

Orlando mounted his horse, and with a kick we were off. He was a taciturn fellow and rode ahead, leaving me to enjoy the illusion of solitude as we trotted across farmlands, splashed through streams, and climbed the rugged trails into sandstone hills.

The view from a horse exceeds that of the best sports utility vehicle—three hundred sixty degrees and unencumbered by roof or glass, with no distraction from engine noises or beeping horns. Since horses watch the ground to assure their footing, riders are free to take in the broader and more distant views. From my saddle, there was much to survey. It was hot but the air was dry and the sky clear, with stunning views in every direction.

We passed oxen pairs pulling creaky wooden plows that cut through dirt the color of rust. *Guajiros* shouted melodic commands that the animals but not I could understand. Their voices echoed across the fields as blue and brown butterflies blinked by. Pigs wallowed and squealed in a muddy stream next to a young boy fishing. He held up his silvery catch for us to see. Huge kapok trees spread their branches like fingers against the *mogotes* and the blue sky. A calf slept luxuriously under a stand of bamboo. Guinea hens and chickens peeped and scurried away as the hooves of our horses disturbed the brush. Each turn in the trail brought new views of the *mogotes*, mysteriously draped with thick green vegetation and spotted with cave openings and stalactites. In the brilliant sun, the shadows cast by the hills contrasted with the phosphorescent green of rice paddies and tobacco fields.

I slowed to a walk, breathless with the beauty of Cuba, and turned in my saddle, hungry to absorb every speck. From here, international politics felt as remote as the winter snows of Ohio. There were no boundaries of politics or nation, only the ephemeral magnificence of Earth. I was suffused with a sense of the privilege of my life and knew in that moment that whatever purported agenda I thought had drawn me to Cuba was self-deception, cover for more fundamental needs. The freedom to explore and have an adventure alone and of my own choosing, the opportunity to be encircled by the splendor of the Cuban countryside as in the arms of God: these were the gifts I had come searching for.

Before ascending the final stretch to the edge of the community of *acuáticos*, Orlando gestured for me to wait. An inspector frequented the area, and Orlando needed to check to make sure he was not around. Riding on these trails was forbidden, he explained, because they could be treacherous to the horses. Orlando gave his mount a swift kick and I watched his magenta cap bob toward the horizon. My horse cooled in the shade while I rested. I thought his explanation a bit odd and wondered what would happen if we were caught trespassing.

An hour passed before I heard the clopping of Orlando's horse galloping down the trail toward me. Orlando waved.

"¡Adelante!" he called. Coast clear.

The final approach was rocky and steep. The sun was high. Green and fertile fields spread below us, shadowed by *mogotes* and tobacco barns the color of cigars. We arrived at a modest wooden home, still under construction and situated to take advantage of the view. Orlando called and a woman in a black T-shirt appeared and gestured for us to dismount. She was young and nondescript, probably in her twenties. We followed her into her almost empty house where we sat on slatted wooden chairs on a bare slab floor.

She was quiet and passive, neither interested in talking nor interesting to talk with.

"Do you use medicines?" I asked.

"No, just water."

"Special water?"

"No, just water."

"Any water?" I pushed.

"Yes. Any water. The water in the faucet will do."

"Are you aware of shortages of medicine in Cuba?"

"No," she replied, looking bored. She shifted her weight back in her rocking chair. Not even my best attempts to engage her drew out more than a monosyllabic response. I wished I had constructed a formal interview, something to move us from the pedestrian to the substantive. Margaret Mead would have elicited richer responses but I could not. After ten minutes or so, I stopped trying. The woman rose and briefly disappeared into another room. When she returned, she handed me a halved green fruit that I didn't recognize and a cup of rice wine, then sat back down and lapsed into talking with Orlando. I ate the mushy fruit in silence, feeling disappointed both in her and in myself—I couldn't tell the difference. This wasn't what I had hoped for.

My hands were sticky with the sugary juice. I interrupted her conversation with Orlando to ask if I could wash my hands. She directed me to an outside spigot where I scrubbed and splashed my face with the water. Just in case the *acuáticos* were right, I took a few sips.

Wet.

Orlando said it was time to leave. I dared hope that the next *acuático* I met would be more engaging. I offered the woman a dollar in recognition of her obvious need and the business-like manner in which she had proffered hospitality. She matter-of-factly accepted it as if this happened every day, and I realized that maybe this cross-cultural encounter did occur in this home every day. Without thinking, I had unwittingly assumed the role of Tourist, making a pilgrimage to find the elusive exotic and willing to pay my way with American dollars. She played her part too, assuming the role of Other for a tip that would help her buy food.

I was in the midst of such musings when Orlando announced that it was too late to go higher into the hills. We had been delayed too long by the need to avoid the inspector and besides, he explained, a meal was being prepared for me back in the valley. I felt another wave of disappointment. This very ordinary woman would be the only *acuático* I would meet.

Having no choice, I remounted for the descent. It wasn't long before the grey clouds of unmet expectation were cleared by the sensual pleasure of being on horseback again—the pungent equine scent and the familiar squeaks, swooshes, and clops of jeans meeting leather meeting horse meeting ground.

~

We emerged from the hills into a scattering of farms. At a white clapboard house with a thatched roof, we dismounted and Orlando introduced me to a slender young woman named Rosa and her 11-year-old daughter Lucita, then left, reminding me that Silvio would come for me later. Rosa invited me inside. Lucita followed closely, looking shyly at me with deep-set eyes just like her mother's, the color of dark chocolate and the shape of almonds. Their home was pristine; the wood, inside and out, freshly painted the color of milk. A bookshelf loaded with colorful ceramic figurines separated the living room from a small eating area. Hand-sewn curtains covered the bedroom doorways, and a sewing machine sat in the corner.

Rosa smiled. She was gap-toothed. Unlike her daughter, she had dark shadows under her eyes and carried herself with a weariness not entirely hidden by her hospitality. She invited me to sit at a table made festive with a flowered tablecloth, and served me fried *malanga* chips, boiled potatoes, a potage of black beans, rice, a fricassee made with a chicken she had raised, and sweet coffee. From where I sat, an open window framed two emerald *mogotes* that poked at right angles out of chartreuse fields. Chickens hurried by, and a pig briefly entered the doorway, oinked, and charged out again.

As Rosa cleared the table, I asked her what I owed her for the meal. *"Lo que quiera,"* she replied, whatever you want. She had been hired to feed me by the man who owned the horses. She would give him whatever I paid, and he would keep *"lo que quiera"*—whatever *he* wanted—and let her keep the change. I put a five dollar bill on the table and asked her what she would use her portion for.

"Zapatos," she said, showing me the shredded black sneakers on her feet, *"y jabón."* Good soap, the kind you can only buy with dollars. Usually she had no choice but to do her laundry with the soap made from beef tallow and lye that she purchased in pesos for the equivalent of forty cents. She left the room and returned shortly with a large white cube which she placed on the table beside me.

"This soap is very, very harsh," she explained, her voice heavy with resignation. She grasped the waxy block in her hand. "When I don't have dollars to buy good soap, I have to choose between wearing dirty clothes or washing them, knowing the soap will open up tiny holes in the fabric," Rosa said, "and this peso soap is too strong for bathing so sometimes I don't." She held out her hands. Her fingernails were dirty from the ash of her wood-burning stove and edged with webs of slivery cuts from doing the family laundry.

She sat down and pulled her daughter into her lap. Lucita, content in her mother's embrace, listened as we talked on. Rosa had never been to Havana; the largest city she had visited was Pinar del Rio where she had given birth to her four children in the hospital. Her husband worked the land and supplied much of the food for the household. He only occasionally earned cash, almost always in pesos. Life was difficult for them but she was proud of how her family shared and how Cubans helped one another.

Rosa looked at her daughter, lovingly. "I want her to become a teacher or a doctor, to have a better life than mine." She paused. "The people in your country struggle and work hard and you get this," she said, pointing to the bill I had left on the table. "We just struggle and work hard." I sensed no anger in her words. She was just stating what was.

It was time to leave. I thought about how hard life was for Rosa's family without regular access to either tourist dollars or relatives in the States and how easy my life was, with money, time for discretionary travel, and nothing approaching soap worries. When she wasn't looking, I tucked an extra two dollars under the tablecloth for her to discover later. I took pictures of Rosa and Lucita with their arms around each other. Lucita wrote down their address hoping I would send pictures to them. As Rosa and I parted, we kissed each other on both cheeks. "You have a house in Cuba. Come back. I feed you. You pay nothing."

I climbed into Silvio's taxi in slow motion: my legs were horse-weary. The seat felt luxurious after bumping along in the saddle and sitting on wooden chairs. I nestled in, spent. In contrast, Silvio appeared as fresh and energetic as when he had picked me up in the morning. During the trip back to Pinar del Rio, I asked him to explain the financial and legal logistics of our day's excursion.

Silvio said he was driving me around illegally and was regularly fined by the *policía* for consorting with tourists. "But," he explained, "the greater the risk, the better the economics." Paying occasional fines, equivalent to what I paid him for the day, was routine. The man who rented his horses did so illegally since only the state was permitted to do so. Orlando had been paid illegally by the horse owner since it was illegal for any one person to hire another. According to Silvio, if caught, both the guide and the owner would have been fined and the horses confiscated. No wonder Orlando was worried about being seen by an inspector; his claim that horses were forbidden was a decoy for his real concern.

"Did you get a commission for bringing them my business?" I asked.

"No," he responded, "but Orlando gave me a bag of yucca because we are friends."

There was more. Rosa's lunch was an illegal transaction since she was hired by the horse owner. Silvio assured me—although I wasn't convinced—that these activities put Cubans at risk but not the foreigners whom they assisted. Everything, he said, had been done illegally, *por la izquierda.* To use the expression "by the left" to refer to clandestine and forbidden activities struck me as perversely funny in a country already leaning so far left as to topple over.

I asked Silvio if he ever bribed the police officers. No, he said, that might happen in Havana, but in Pinar it would only get you into more trouble. As we spoke, he saw a police car stopped by the side of the road ahead of us. *"No se preocupe,*" he said. Don't worry. With eyes glued to the road ahead, we sped by, and the *policía* became a mere speck in the rearview mirror.

Phil arrived back at Cheche's about the same time I did. Quiet by nature, he was more talkative than usual about the day he had spent with his group. He had toured the school attended by Rosa's children. He was excited as he shared what he had seen, state-of-the-art solar panels providing energy for basic school equipment—a television, a computer, and lights, "green" technology being used throughout the country, even in one-room school houses with fewer than a half-dozen students. He thought he might install a demonstration Cuban solar unit in his classroom at home.

We had each enjoyed our separate excursions, his within the guidelines of the tour group, mine in collusion with Silvio the rule bender. Memories of the day reverberated inside me: the thrill of riding horseback among the *mogotes*, the lovely openness of Rosa and her family, a myriad of transcendent moments amidst a landscape of unforgettable splendor. Clearly, life outside the rules—*por la izquierda*—had its rewards.

What I went looking for was not to be found, but the unexpected grandeur of the Cuban countryside had dwarfed all disappointment. I seemed to need the same lesson repeatedly. To thrive, I needed to slow down and stop obsessing about goals. Projecting rigid expectations and scrambling frantically after them put me at risk of missing the very experiences that I most treasured. No wonder I had felt sapped of energy in my academic life. I'd been galloping along like a horse wearing blinders, oblivious to what was beyond my narrow view.

The next morning, as Cheche served us coffee, eggs, and fresh pineapple, she said there was something she needed to discuss with us. She looked worried. The evening before, she had overheard the tail end of my discussion with Silvio about the financial and legal aspects of our excursion. She was concerned about what might come up in further conversation. Silvio would be stopping by later, she said, her voice low, and—just in case he asked—could we tell him that we were only paying her ten dollars a night instead of twenty and that we had arrived on Tuesday instead of Monday? Yes, he was a friend, she emphasized, but he was also the inspector for her rental and what she had to pay him depended on her income. Cheche cooked the books.

chapter 18

It was a bittersweet departure. Phil and I were returning to Ohio together, and it wouldn't be long before our daughter would be home for the summer. My cross-cultural energies were depleted and I was eager for my own cooking, coffee with my village buddies, and—I confess—even a trip to the mall. I looked forward to seeing my parents and siblings at our annual family reunion. But I knew that it would be a stretch from May until December when I would be back in Cuba for the religious pilgrimage and my stay at the convent—too long. And between now and then loomed the ominous expectation that I return to my job.

In August my sabbatical ended and I re-entered the life of the university. My cadence had slowed during the months away and I had discovered that a steady trot—with regular breaks for friends, reading, and exercise—was much more conducive to peace of mind than the lurch and frenzy that had been my style before taking leave. Unfortunately, this horse and buggy was headed back to the LA freeway; I felt the pressure to merge with the traffic and resume the local speed.

My responsibilities were the same, the office politics were the same, and the cast of characters was the same as before I'd left. Only I wasn't. I'd expanded into a bigger life. Hard as I tried, I couldn't settle down. My office felt like a cage and I, like a barely-domesticated animal compelled to pace between the corners of my confinement as if there were an escape if only I could find it. Emails popped onto my computer screen with a polite "I look forward to hearing about Cuba and your travels," but curiosity rarely materialized in person. No one at work could mirror the changed parts of me, nor did they care to. Returning from Peace Corps thirty years earlier had felt like this: reverse culture shock, the collision of intense experience abroad with indifference at home.

Some of my old patients returned and a few new ones called for appointments. At times their concerns struck me as trivial and the money they paid me as extravagant. My mind was populated with Cubans coping with more serious problems, Cubans for whom my hourly psychotherapy fee represented a three month salary. I thought of Rosa struggling to find the dollars needed to buy soap that wouldn't eat her clothes, of the sisters who cleaned leprous wounds without gloves because they didn't have any, and of a psychologist I had met who was unable to obtain the anti-psychotic medicine that helped her schizophrenic sister. Whether the stimulus was a note from Enrique or an unusually hot summer day, my attentions were easily hijacked to Cuba.

Phone calls, meetings, and emails nudged me to reassume responsibilities that I had gladly fled months earlier. I felt as if I were being asked to dress myself out of a laundry bag of dirty clothes. Needing the employment until I could figure out an alternative life, I faked interest and engagement, working on the admissions committee, preparing lectures, conferring with other faculty about manuscripts and research projects. Survival was all, honesty a luxury I couldn't afford. I counted the weeks and months until December and my last planned trip to the island, clasping onto some inchoate hope that this final trip would bring the answer to the obvious question that my academic life had become.

In October an excited email from Enrique announced that he would be spending the month of November in Boston, doing research in the stacks of the Harvard libraries under a special grant to support Cuban scholars. Elated for him but thinking about Massachusetts cold, I gathered gloves, wool socks, and Phil's old winter parka, and mailed a package to Cambridge to warm his welcome.

A week after his arrival, I called him. He was cozy in the clothes I had sent, feasting on the extravagant offerings of the university archives, and copying as much material as he could possibly carry home. I imagined another tower of papers claiming space in his apartment. But his life outside the library stacks was spare and unsatisfying. To buy a cup of coffee in Harvard Square was beyond his budget, and he was finding New Englanders as chilly as the weather. I could hear the travel loneliness in his voice and thought of all the times his kindness had soothed mine. "Come to Ohio for the weekend," I suggested, hoping to tempt him. "We will buy your ticket."

"I couldn't," he said. Economic inequality was an irritant I wanted to brush aside. *"El mundo no es justo, amigo."* The world isn't just. "Just come."

When we picked him up at the airport in our red Volvo, he greeted us as family. He was as excited to make the acquaintance of our car as to see us, smitten with her heated seats and push-button windows as if she were a new lover.

Phil and I did our best to fill the weekend with experiences Enrique wouldn't have in Havana. I took him to buy groceries at our local supermarket, modest by North American standards. I was unloading the bags into the kitchen cupboards when Phil arrived home, weighed down with groceries from his own spontaneous spree. We had each done the shopping without consulting the other. Enrique looked on as we assessed our duplications on the kitchen counter: two cartons of eggs, two gallons of milk, meat for an army, and bags and bags of fruits and vegetables. I began formulating an explanation, but stopped, trusting Enrique to absorb what was readily apparent: we could afford two sets of groceries, food was easily available, and our marital roles weren't clearly defined.

The next morning we woke to a dusting of snow and Enrique looked out the frosty windows in wonder. He asked us to take a picture of him on our front deck, bundled up in Phil's blue parka and standing on a thin sheet of ice sprinkled with snowflakes too small to be visible in the photo.

We visited the homes of our close friends so that he could see a sampling of houses and life styles and get a sense of our social world. We stopped by my office at the local family medicine clinic so he could see our version of a *consultorio.* And we made a special stop at the local dairy where high school students in red uniforms scooped heaps of ice cream into shakes and cones for a never-ending line of obese Ohioans. The dairy kept a herd of goats and sold brown kibble from coin-operated dispensers so that patrons could feed the entertaining menagerie. A quarter slipped in the slot released a handful.

"Súper-capitalismo," I explained, as the goats nibbled the pellets from Enrique's hand. I felt strangely proud of the entrepreneurial excess of my culture.

Late in the afternoon we returned home and relaxed with glasses of wine by a roaring fire in a living room that would have swallowed his whole apartment. Our golden retriever settled in the just-right spot to toast her fur. Feet up, we spoke of our children—each of us having an "only." Enrique had wanted to meet Karin but she was away at college.

"We really miss her for the months that she's away," I said. "I imagine it is hard for you to be separate from Belkis and Enriquito when you travel."

"¿Sí, cómo no?" he replied. His comments ambled toward other parental concerns. "Sometimes I fear that Enriquito will disappear overnight, that he and his friends will leave Cuba as *balseros*," he said, quietly. That Enrique could understand the urge made it seem all the more plausible. There were so many opportunities and material goods in the United States that young people in Cuba didn't have—cars, for example. Unless Enriquito landed a state job that required and provided an automobile, it would be impossible for him to get one. Even if he could, there would be the matter of fuel. Enrique sounded worried. "Enriquito and his friends just want to know what it's like to drive."

His comments saddened me. We were speaking not of economic abstractions but of particulars that kept him up at night. I remembered Karin turning sixteen and our anxious pleasure as she began to drive Big Blue—the old box of a Volvo that served as our second car. Neither the availability of wheels nor the expense of gas had been an issue. I thought about the concerns I still carried for her—that she find a career and a partner that suited her. They felt minor in contrast with Enrique's. I didn't have to worry about Karin risking her life to flee the country or having her career options limited by government decree.

Beneath the comfort of familial closeness that Enrique and I shared, tugged tensions: on my side guilt and relief, on his, envy and resentment. Or so I imagined—none were directly expressed. That we could diplomatically dance on such ambivalent ground was a measure of our friendship.

On Sunday morning, I took Enrique for coffee with the old guys at the village café. When we arrived, a dozen men were already crowded around the table under a map of Cuba. Bill had suggested that I bring in a map so that the group could keep track of my whereabouts, and it had hung there on the wall for months. The men greeted Enrique in entry-level Spanish and offered him a chair in their circle. I brought him a cup of coffee with plenty of sugar. Stan, the retired chemistry professor, engaged him in a discussion about science teaching and Enrique's English rose to the occasion. There was talk back and forth about the war on terrorism, life in the village, and the embargo of Cuba. It was people-to-people diplomacy of the sweetest kind. For a spell, with Enrique in our midst, the Florida Straits were of no consequence.

part 4

pilgrimage

chapter 19

What do you pack for a stay with sisters in a convent at a leprosy sanatorium? One suitcase I stuffed with medical supplies—bandages, procedure trays, mega-bottles of acetaminophen, and more latex gloves. Remembering Sor Carmen's face when I had given her chocolate buckeyes, I tucked in another box. A second suitcase had to accommodate clothes and toiletries for a month, my personal papers and books, and a briefcase-worth of copied articles that Enrique had asked me to carry, the overflow from his Harvard stint. Having no experience with sleeping arrangements in a convent, I added a bathrobe to my usually scant travel wardrobe. Wondering what their fate would be, I slipped a half-dozen new pairs of ladies' underpants into the corners. I'd bought them on sale for $1.99 each, knowing they would make precious gifts. Several were patterned with blue stars, others with red hearts.

No matter how many trips I had under my belt, the psychological transition was never easy. On the verge of leaving husband, hearth, and home, I inevitably stumbled into an anxiety-filled pit that churned with irrational fears of impending accident or calamity. Climbing out usually took days rather than hours, especially when travel involved multiple flights and—as was the case this time—staying overnight in an anonymous airport hotel along the way. Between home and away I often wondered whether the journey would be worth the emotional cost. What sustained me was the knowledge that I always felt this way and that as I approached Cuba the pain of separation would be eclipsed by the pleasure of arrival.

When I peered down at Toronto after takeoff, the grey landscape had the pinkish cast of dead meat. Three and a half hours later, lush green rose toward me, speckled with creamy blips of buildings that enlarged with our descent. When the airplane wheels bounced and touched down on the tarmac of the José Martí airport, I felt as if Cuba were laying hands on me in blessing.

~

Emerging from Customs, I spotted Enrique and Belkis all smiles and waves over the mesh fence that separated the new arrivals from the waiting crowds. The arrival area was bursting with emotion. Cuban Americans who had been on my flight eagerly pressed toward the gate as family members called to them with tears streaming down their faces. Restrictions that limited family visits to once a year meant that I was seeing my "family" more often than blood relatives typically saw theirs. We pushed through the gate to the pleasure of waiting hugs and kisses.

Enrique grabbed my bags and minutes later I was settled into the back of their Moskavitch. The front seats were freshly adorned with new cotton slipcovers. Belkis had recently painted the whole car a luminous lime green and hennaed her dark brown hair a luminous red. The colors were harbingers of Christmas.

Since Enrique had left our house just days before, our conversation had barely been interrupted. When he had been our guest, our talk had focused on his experience in the United States. Now on his turf, my first query elicited his detailed description of the economic situation since my last visit. Life was harder. There were more scarcities. Produce in the farmers' markets was more expensive. And less food was provided by the state; the milk rations for small children had been reduced.

As Enrique spoke my eyes darted out the windows looking for the familiar political slogans that lined the highway from the airport to Havana. I needed them to be there to reassure me that capitalism hadn't gobbled up the island while I'd been gone.

"No one can take away our hope!"

"We will continue to conquer with patience, ideas, effort, and heroism!"

"Che lives!"

Their absurd appeal hadn't worn off, and I was giddy with delight.

Within a half hour we arrived at Enrique's tree-shaded corner of Vedado. I had planned to stay with Ibis and Estelle, but when my reservation was preempted by a previous guest extending his visit, Enrique had rescued me by arranging for another *casa particular*. This time I would stay with an elderly couple who lived in a large house catty-corner to his apartment. I hoped he would collect a finder's fee, though I didn't embarrass him by asking.

My hosts were an odd pair. Armando was eighty and moved in perpetual slow motion—fixing, hauling, or adjusting whatever his wife insisted that he fix, haul or adjust. His head was always down in submissive resignation as he ambled about the property in passive good humor. The matron of the house was Pirina, a name that I could recall only by cueing myself with the word *"aspirina."* Her hair was black with *canas*—a funny word for gray or white hair—that almost touched her shoulders. Gravity and sunshine had added heaviness to her features, but she was still lovely.

Each morning as she prepared breakfast for me, Pirina wore the same outfit as she had the day before: a red printed dress that hung from elastic just above her breasts and left her shoulders bare, and a green and red floral shirt. Her daily breakfasts were ever the same too. The morning ritual began with her handing me a small cup of opaque black coffee saturated with sugar. Before the cup reached my lips, she held out her hand in expectation and chirped *"¿Ya?"* as Dulce had done months earlier, and I would tighten my grip, still preferring to sip than slug. Then came the spread—scrambled eggs with ham, fresh papaya, two pieces of dry toast, a glass of fresh squeezed orange juice, and *café con leche*. She provided abundant nourishing food that I knew not to take for granted, for a sign in front of a neighborhood restaurant announced, *"No hay ni café ni nada."* There is neither coffee nor anything. Nevertheless, I soon felt regimented in her care. After the first few days, the eggs tasted saltier and saltier, and even eating the papaya, which I loved, started to feel like an onerous requirement. I began to understand why Armando hung his head.

My room was an adequately furnished cell, short on windows and aesthetics. The only door opened onto the patio and was covered with an iron grill that, when closed and locked, invited fresh air while maintaining security. From the doorway I could see across the patio and the street and tell when Enrique's front door was open.

~

Crossing the street one afternoon to his open door, I found Enrique, phone in hand, sitting in his usual black chair in the corner of the *sala.* He was talking loudly with a colleague while rap music pulsed from the stereo he had just brought back from the United States for his son's birthday. I sat on the short sofa across from him, our knees almost bumping. Belkis offered me a *cafecito* and then disappeared into the recesses of the apartment.

While Enrique finished his call, I sipped coffee and observed this man who had come to feel like a brother. He was wearing shorts and a T-shirt with a red, white, and blue Puerto Rican flag on the front. Although he had told me that he wished he didn't smoke, he was puffing on an unfiltered Cuban cigarette, knocking the ashes into one of seven ashtrays that circled a vase of plastic purple flowers beside him.

The *sala* was visually congested, every surface an excuse for decoration. A miniature artificial Christmas tree stood on a side table next to him. Red and yellow lights flashed amid the green fir branches, keeping beat with the music. The tree leaned against a wall mirror that magnified the dance and dazzle of the lights and the pounding of the music. A ceramic tile depicting a river scene in France hung above the tree and next to a mahogany cuckoo clock garnished with silver metallic birds. Looking over all, from a high ledge, was a figure that appeared to be the Virgin Mary, white-skinned, blue-robed, and angelic. In fact, she was not the Virgin but a saint, Enrique explained, although he couldn't tell me which one. The painted wooden figure dated from the late nineteenth century and was the gift of a friend who had left for the United States. The saint's hair was real. Once when he was out of earshot, Belkis confided that Enrique sometimes removed the miniature wig and washed it.

On the wall behind me hung a Native American mask and a painting of the Pope being embraced by a haloed Virgin. Above the Pope was an oil painting showing the whole of Cuba, "the pearl of the Antilles," floating in a blue sea, dwarfed by a huge fish flying overhead and straddled by three bare-breasted ladies.

Enrique's living space was a metaphor for his situation, the contents too compressed, his ambitions too large, for the constraints of his environment. He needed space to stretch, more than his home—or his country—could provide. How ironic, I thought, that I had traded a suffocating professional situation at home for the experience of a country that imposed so many limitations on its citizens.

The evening news blared from the television in the corner. It was the usual news: good news about Cuba, bad news about the rest of the world, sports, and weather. A middle-aged woman in thick dark-framed glasses who wouldn't have made the first cut for a newscaster position in the United States, announced the fortieth anniversary of the arrival of *Granma*, the boat that had transported Fidel and his men from Mexico to the mountainous shores of eastern Cuba and revolution.

To Enrique's left, I could see into the dining area where bookcases stacked tight with old yellowed tomes consumed half of the floor space. Over his right shoulder, I peered through his bedroom door to piles of books and papers that framed the computer monitor on his desk. On his old computer, cramped between bed and books, he could send and receive email, his window to Not Cuba.

Many Cubans would consider Enrique a lucky man. Few had the opportunity to travel abroad, and, as an academic physician, at least he could petition the state for permission to attend international meetings or conduct research abroad but never with his family, never with adequate financial resources, never without a pre-approved agenda. My resources and freedoms loomed large in comparison—OFAC restrictions notwithstanding.

My mind wandered, and I dared imagine my own luckier version of a fuller life. It would be a one that entailed taking more chances. I would leave the university once and for all and travel more, to Cuba, of course—I had become too connected not to—but elsewhere in Latin America too. And I would write. Not dry articles for obscure academic journals—I had produced enough of those—but richer prose, fertilized with the compost of my experience. I wouldn't give up my psychologist role completely. There would be therapy patients in this imagined new life, but a modest number and only those who could tolerate my comings and goings. With our daughter's college graduation not far off, tuition payments would soon be over, and I wouldn't have to stay in my academic position. Besides, if my spirits flourished, life on a tighter budget might not feel like a sacrifice. What besides lack of gumption and an insane loyalty to a claustrophobically limiting job kept me from leaping with both feet into my own bigger life?

chapter 20

The rhythms of the drums and calabashes reverberated through the house in celebration of the fiesta for Changó, the deity of fire, passion, and music. Within the Afro-Cuban religion of *santería,* drumming was the means human beings used to communicate with the various African guardian spirits—*orishas* or *santos,* as they were called. I was enjoying this *toque de tambores* at a private home in Luyanó, a poor neighborhood on the southern outskirts of Havana. The *sala* of the simple wooden abode was filled with drummers and dancers and onlookers pressed around the edges, while front windows framed the smiling wide-eyed faces of neighborhood children who jostled each other for better views.

A *norteamericana* percussionist and Cuba regular, whom I had met in the patio of the Hotel Nacional, had invited me to this celebration at the family home of Leandro, her drumming instructor. The evening promised to introduce me to serious practitioners of *santería.* I was curious. From Gary I had learned that the vast majority of Cubans practiced some form of this Afro-Cuban religion, more than followed any other religious tradition, and I knew that spiritual beliefs often shaped how people interpreted their bodily experience and treated health problems.

Santería had its roots in the late 1700s when the Spanish colonialists brought shiploads of Yoruba slaves from Nigeria to the Caribbean islands and forced Catholicism on them along with labor in the sugar plantations. In creative refusal to relinquish their heritage, the slaves continued their African religious beliefs and practices, disguising them in the protective cloak of Catholicism. Each *orisha* spirit became linked with a Catholic saint in the syncretism of *santería.* The double-identities enabled the slaves to honor their African deities even while "converting" to Catholicism.

In accepting the invitation, I hoped that the evening might prepare me for the pilgrimage to San Lázaro later in the month. I had learned that the pilgrimage celebrated the Catholic tradition and honored Saint Lázarus, the patron saint for lepers reputed to heal the sick, but that on a more subterranean level the pilgrimage reflected *santería* beliefs and honored the *orisha* Babalú Ayé. Many Cubans, especially those of African descent, hedged their bets by nodding to both traditions, but on this particular night, people were pushed to assert a preference; festivities at this house in Luyanó would be in honor of Changó, one of the most venerated *santos* of the Yoruba cult, and the celebrants were practitioners of *santería,* while in other locations, at the same time, Catholics would be honoring Santa Barbara.

When the *taxista* dropped me off in Luyanó, I thought I must have given him the wrong address. The white house with peeling paint looked completely closed up. I ventured to knock anyway and was surprised when the front door opened and I was greeted by Leandro's octogenarian father, Alfredo. He was a robust and friendly fellow in a shimmering scarlet tunic with a mandarin collar. "Come in, come in," he said, his right arm outstretched. "You are first but others will arrive shortly."

Red and white were the colors of the day—Changó's colors. Without conscious awareness, I had dressed in a khaki skirt and rose-colored shirt, the closest approximation that my suitcase contained. My colors were subdued next to those of my flamboyant host, Alfredo, who had proudly donned pressed white trousers, white belt, and spotless white shoes for the occasion. A gold medallion of the Virgin dangled from a chain around his neck, set off by his bronze skin. A red beret that matched his silk shirt tilted rakishly across his bald head. He projected the virility associated with his *santo,* and I didn't mind looking.

Alfredo beamed, put an arm around my shoulder, and drew me into his home. He introduced me to his wife, a dark woman in white who must have been equally stunning in her youth, then gestured toward an altar to Changó that filled a whole corner of the room. A glorious array of fruits and sweets and flowers covered a cloth mat on the floor: a basket toppling with fresh fruit, a stand of freshly cut plantains, a bouquet of white daisies and pink gladiolas, a round cake covered in blue and white frosting, a plate heaped with fluffy meringues, and several bowls of foods I couldn't identify. Affixed to the wall above this tribute and below a figure of *La Virgen de la Caridad del Cobre* hung a red brocade cloth embossed with gold thread, folded and arranged in a human form to represent the *orisha.* A dish for offerings sat next to a red gourd rattle. Discerning that I didn't know what to do next, Alfredo suggested that I shake the rattle at the altar and ask Changó for *"salud."*

I was feeling healthier than I had in months. My shoulder had mended well. My Sjogren's symptoms of dry eyes and achiness had abated significantly with trips south. And while returning to my university position had required internal gymnastics, anticipating this December trip had buoyed me up sufficiently to keep me in safe enough waters. Nonetheless, I didn't hesitate to petition Changó for health—for myself and for Cuba. Ecumenically, I placed a bill in the dish.

Alfredo's house was spacious, with white walls, high ceilings and brown wooden beams. Within a few minutes a gaggle of guys with drums and gourds arrived, gathering in the *sala* where they leaned their instruments against the wall near the tribute to Changó. There was a rumble of women in the dining area making preparations for eating. A chicken had been sacrificed for the occasion, thankfully before my arrival. More guests streamed in, arriving in twos and threes until three generations of Alfredo's lineage and friends filled his home. All were Cuban, and the friend who had invited me was nowhere to be seen.

The drumming started, slowly at first. Leandro, the drumming instructor, energetically thumped a tall Congo drum which he gripped between his knees. Next to him, his baby brother and another teenager in Changó red accompanied him on theirs. The drum skins had been tapped and slapped to a brown patina, still eggshell white at the rims. Conversation competed with the musical staccato of drums and dance.

Leandro's wife Georgina, her body all angles and her white dress all curves, swooped and dipped, waving her hands in front of her, appearing to fall and catch herself with the rise and fall of the percussive beats. A turban tightly wrapped around her head matched the honey of her skin and marked her status as a *santera*, a priestess. Others danced but only Georgina held the audience. Watching her compelled me to the periphery of the group where I stood awkwardly. I have always been drawn to rhythm; Aretha Franklin's *Respect* set the sonorous beat for my college years. But translating rhythm to dance never came easily, even in a situation less foreign. Whenever my eyes met Alfredo's, we smiled at each other, but I felt uncharacteristically shy, immobilized by the mix of his friendly attractiveness and the overall strangeness of the scene.

The booming escalated until the cacophonous crescendo made all but nonverbal communication impossible. I should have guessed when I saw the old woman shimmy onto the dance floor what would come next. Both her appearance and her behavior set her apart. In a crowd that covered the color spectrum, she was coal black. Her turban was white, her deep brown eyes bloodshot. Marigold yellow patches splotched her black dress and glowed electric as she vibrated and jerked to the thrumming drums. Others danced and then rested, but she pressed on, gyrating and whirling until her skin was a glossy sheen and drops of sweat flew from her. Her eyes rolled back behind half-closed lids and she looked like she might lose her balance.

Georgina and the other dancers moved to the sides of the room to give her space. The drumsticks thumped louder and louder against the skins of the Congo drums. When it seemed the erotic percussion could build no further, it climaxed, jolting a young male dancer forward toward the frenzied woman, yelling at her aggressively in a language I couldn't comprehend—Yoruba? Suspense stifled my breathing. I watched him menace her until—SMASH—it was as if she had crashed through a pane of glass and with a paroxysm of wild abandon emerged a different person on the other side, possessed.

Her eyes glazed, fixated at some distant point. "Elegua," Georgina whispered to me, identifying the *orisha* now inhabiting the entranced woman. Elegua, a mischievous *orisha* with powers of healing and clairvoyance, was feared and revered, reputed to live behind the door and entrusted to open and close paths. The woman seemed to be grasping at the air, as if trying to get her bearings.

When I lifted my camera to take pictures as I had earlier in the evening, Georgina gestured no, laying her long arm across the front of my body.

"Not now," she hushed. "I will tell you when you can again. She may speak to you, if she has something to say."

Riveted, I waited. She stopped dancing and assumed the role of trickster. I couldn't see where she got her supplies but the next minute she was tying a scarf around her waist, puffing on a large cigar and carrying a bottle of rum. The atmosphere had changed from somber to playful, and she weaved among the guests, engaging one, then another in magical antics. She offered one man a sip of rum from her bottle, only to pull it away the moment his lips touched the glass, leaving him open-mouthed and dry. She approached me and, caught off guard, I too fell for the bottle trick I had just seen her do with another. When I succumbed, she threw her head back and expelled a loud cackling laugh and a cloud of cigar smoke. Suddenly shifting again to a serious mood, she looked directly at me.

"You like to observe as a way to learn things," she said. "And you have a problem with papers of some kind at home, right?"

Shuffling quickly through the deck of problems always on file in my head, I couldn't identify what she might be referring to, though it seemed that my professional life had always been too full of papers. Or perhaps she was referring to the issue of travel licenses to Cuba. Maybe she knew something about OFAC that I didn't. I nodded noncommittally.

"And sometimes you feel tranquil but other times you need to wander alone to have your own thoughts." How very true, I thought. I'd certainly done a lot of that as of late.

"You have two *orishas*, Elegua and Olokun," she went on. Georgina, intuiting my limited knowledge of *santería* matters, leaned toward me. "They represent peace, tranquility, stability and health. Maybe another time, I can teach you more." I knew a bit about Elegua, guardian of the crossroads with the power to usher in new directions, and though I wasn't familiar with Olokun, I was sure I could use the favor of more than one divinity. Later I would learn that Olokun represented the divinity of ocean depths and was often evoked on behalf of healing. Crossroads and healing; she had me pegged.

The old woman continued on her rounds, and I lost track of her in the whirl of guests. Much later in the evening I glimpsed her again. She had retreated to the sidelines where she looked withered and spent, as if the *orisha* had sucked all life out of her. How fluidly had the old woman—under the spell of trance—shed one identity and been subsumed by another one. From years as a psychotherapist and years of being me, I had concluded that it was nearly impossible for most of us to change fundamentals, but she made it look easy. I knew what I wanted to shed: my academic skin. If only it didn't feel so irrevocable.

A few days later I hailed a battered black and yellow cab to return to Luyanó. Georgina and her drummer husband had invited me to visit them to talk more about *santería.*

I settled into the cab. "Are you Canadian?" my driver asked. It was a safe assumption, given the deluge of Canadian tourists every winter.

"No, I'm from the States."

"What state are you from?" he asked.

"Ohio. Do you know it?" I replied.

"No, we Cubans don't have much opportunity to know. This island is a large prison. Even if you are invited to visit another country, who will pay for your expenses? Besides, you would still need to be investigated and approved for travel. If you are not with the Party . . . well, *no es fácil.*"

"Ah, *no es fácil,*" I repeated, hearing the *dicho* for the umpteenth time. "I've sure heard that a lot."

"Yes, it is our slogan and it is true."

I aimed our conversation in another direction. "So, what do you think of your medical system?" I asked.

"*¡Es malísima!* It's very bad. I would prefer to *pay* to see the doctor and *pay* for medicines and then the doctor should be paid a *real* salary."

"Are you a doctor?" I asked, wondering if I'd found another one.

"No, I'm a lawyer. Yes, imagine, a lawyer driving a cab! But as a lawyer I was only earning pesos, the equivalent of twenty dollars a month. I've been driving a cab for three years now. I rent it from the state, and as a *taxista* I can earn fifteen to twenty dollars a *day.*"

Approaching Luyanó, the road turned from intermittently rough to major bumps and ditches. We neared our destination. "Call me if I can help you again," the *taxista* offered, handing me his card. "We are taught to hate you but I have many friends from your county and I know you are a noble people."

Georgina and Leandro looked less festive than when I had seen them last. Leandro was in a threadbare Florida State T-shirt with the sleeves ripped out. Their apartment was a barren sliver of a dwelling, and it occurred to me that they probably hoped that I would offer to pay for training in *santería.* I had heard of such arrangements but kept this thought to myself, knowing there was no chance of my becoming an initiate. Instead, amidst casual conversation, I asked Leandro about the role of this spiritual tradition in staying healthy or curing an illness.

"Ninety nine percent of Cubans practice some form of *santería,*" Leandro said. Elegua, my *orisha* and the same one that had inhabited the *santera* at the celebration, was capable of prescribing remedies for health problems. The *orisha* Osin was even more expert when it came to herbs. "Only some doctors, but certainly not all, are knowledgeable about herbs. You have to confer with the *orishas.*"

"How do *santería* and the medical care provided by the state work together?" I asked, and Leandro responded with a story. "A few years ago, I was in a lot of pain," he said, poking his hand toward his lower abdomen. "I consulted my *ángel de la guardia,* Changó. He told me that I should go to the doctor and get rid of anything that didn't work. I did. The doctor said I had appendicitis and I agreed to surgery and got well."

As was often the case when my Spanish kept me running to catch up, I didn't think to ask what I later wished I had. Exactly what form did Changó's communication take? If my *orishas* were communicating with me, I didn't want to miss their messages.

chapter 21

The morning sun filtered through the iron bars of the window, cutting jags across my bed. From the bump-and-sag mattress I stared up at the cracked stucco ceiling, not ready to face the day. It was Friday the thirteenth and I was about to surrender myself to the Sisters of Charity.

I hadn't slept well. Back in Ohio, I'd been exhilarated at the thought of staying in the convent and witnessing the nearby pilgrimage to the Church of San Lázaro that took place each year. Since early in my Cuba travels, I had been struggling to find a more free-wheeling and exuberant way of being in the world. When I'd said yes to this strange invitation, I imagined that plunging into a situation where I would be surrounded by Catholic sisters, religious pilgrims, and leprosy sufferers, might consolidate my still-fragile sense of expanded possibility. But waking in Havana on the morning I would make the jump to the convent felt more emotionally complicated. I was flooded with second thoughts and, unable to shake apprehensions that the sisters would readily discern that my religious leanings weren't even in the ballpark of Catholicism and that my declared interest in learning about health matters was subterfuge for a more personal agenda.

This would be the culmination of my last planned trip to Cuba. I wavered between the hope that what awaited me in El Rincón would be a climactic adventure and the fear that it might call my bluff. I felt like a three-year-old perched at the top of a terrifying slide, about to be propelled down, ready or not.

Through the wall that separated my room from the kitchen, I heard the shuffle of steps as Pirina prepared breakfast. I would just have time to eat before Enrique came to pick me up. According to the plans that he had worked out with Sor Carmen, the mother superior, I would be staying at the convent for five days. When I arrived, the pilgrims would already be streaming into El Rincón. In addition to their usual responsibilities at the leprosarium, the sisters at the convent would be immersed in attending to the needs of both the pilgrims and of various priests and sisters visiting from other parts of Cuba and abroad.

I had a litany of worries. I had few experiential coordinates to anchor me in the anticipated mélange of sisters, pilgrims, and lepers. Of course that was also the appeal; I was drawn to the very oddness of the mix. The possibilities both exhilarated and rattled me.

Another worry—for this month I was traveling on general license and needed to be able to demonstrate a full schedule of research activity if asked by Homeland Security upon reentry into the States. Heading to a convent for a religious pilgrimage stretched the definition of "research on health care" and threatened my sense of safety. Sure, the pilgrims were on a health mission, perhaps vaguely related to scarcities of medicine resulting from the embargo, and the location of the convent within the perimeter of the leprosy sanatorium provided a medical context. Still, I worried that the immigration authorities might not buy my participant-observer approach as "research" and that I would be perceived as an experience junkie rather than a social scientist.

And even if I didn't get into trouble with my government, I would have to contend with theirs. The vigilant Cuban state didn't permit casual access to its health facilities and I had no official permission to visit the leprosy sanatorium where the convent was located. Anyone who stopped to consider my presence in El Rincón might wonder why I was there, and the authorities—whoever and wherever they were—might nab me for straying too far from the tourist path. I felt as if I were harboring a psychic version of the Cold War, courting cosmic retribution for pushing the rules too far.

Ironically, the thought of living in a nest of nuns was more stressful than the thought of being in close contact with leprosy patients. Years among doctors had accustomed me to illness, but Catholic sisters made me uneasy. When I was a child, my mother told me that the little white marks on my finger nails were caused by little white lies, so when a Catholic classmate in elementary school spoke about "confession," I pictured an all-knowing sister examining the spattering of white on my nails and demanding that I account for my each and every fabrication. Subsequent contact with real nuns had failed to dissipate my apprehensions. When I was a teenager traveling with my family in Europe, we found lodging at a convent in Rome. It was Holy Week and the sisters had taken vows of silence for Lent and didn't mix with the guests. They hovered in the shadows of the convent dining room while I sat between my brother and sister, sipping the watery gruel that passed for food during the sacred weeks. I figured that they knew my transgressions without even looking at my hands.

Strange that in my fifties I was preoccupied with hovering nuns, but Cuba had a way of plowing to the surface of my consciousness all sorts of primitive fears and desires. In this strangest of countries, risk and anxiety had become my daily companions, and I often felt like a living demonstration of "regression under stress" from one of my psychology texts. In the uneasy process of finding my way on new ground, my emotional skin easily prickled with childish fears.

As edgy as I felt, I wouldn't have traded my emotional state for what it had been prior to my sabbatical leave when my life had felt like a windowless room too crowded with junk for comfortable habitation. Taking risks and pushing through fear had blown out the walls and I loved the new space and the fresh air. Yes, as I said I would, I had learned about health care and the effects of the embargo, but the more valuable knowledge gained had been more personal. I learned that serendipitous human encounters compelled and satisfied me more than anything academic that I was accomplishing. I learned that when I mustered the courage to stay flexible and relinquish fixed goals, failure in one pursuit offered the freedom to explore others. Most of all I learned that—with loosened ties to home and profession—I could thrive.

I no longer felt claustrophobic in my own skin. I had traded depression for anxiety and relished the exchange; the testing of nerve was the toll required for this journey. So when Enrique said that Sor Carmen had invited me to stay at the convent, I hadn't hesitated. To decline would have meant retreat. Still, on the verge of getting what I really wanted, the chance to engage in a consummate challenge, my chest constricted with uneasiness and (could this be?) guilt. Yes, guilt. And I *was* guilty, guilty of not only *wanting* too much but of *acting* on my longings, mine the double transgression of impulse and action. I felt like a Bad Girl grabbing more cookies than my share off the plate of life.

~

Not wanting to miss a cup of Pirina's *café con leche* finally pulled me out of bed. Enrique had suggested that we leave right after breakfast. The drive from Havana to the village of El Rincón and the convent would only take an hour, but his old Moskavitch was unreliable and he wanted to leave before the heat of the day.

I rose and made my way into the tiny bathroom. With typical Cuban ingenuity, the shower head had been mounted directly above the toilet to save space, presenting a postural challenge to bathing and guaranteeing that I would have a wet bottom if I showered first. *Es Cuba,* I thought. The inconvenience was offset by the pleasure of sampling the quotidian absurdities of life in this place. I made do with the strange configuration and then dressed.

Putting my nightgown and toiletries in my suitcase, I wondered if I had packed what I would need. I'd thrown in a long skirt and several modest blouses, thinking these would be suitable for convent wear or attending mass. Should I have brought something to cover my head? Would it be obvious to the sisters that I was a child of the sixties? Trying to pass as—what?—Catholic? Each question that floated to the surface of my mind brought another one in tow. Where would I sleep? Would I be expected to share a room with the sisters? I imagined an austere dormitory with two rows of beds, a sour-faced sister in black and white habit crisply tucked into each. They must wear pajamas, I thought, but my mind balked at the mental image of sisters undressing. I was glad that I had brought a long nightgown and robe—armor against the unforeseeable.

Over the ever-the-same coffee and eggs and papaya and toast, I told Pirina that I was leaving for El Rincón to witness the pilgrimage to San Lázaro.

"Ah, San Lázaro," she repeated in staccato speech that I found barely understandable. Her wrinkled face seemed to lengthen with longing. She disappeared briefly into the adjoining room and returned with a picture in a wooden frame. There he was, San Lázaro, patron saint of the sick, kind-faced, in purple and white robes and leaning on crutches. Two dogs at his sides licked the wounds on his legs. He was reputed to have been a leper mentioned by Jesus and to have healing powers. As I would soon see for myself, each year he inspired masses of Cubans to extraordinary displays of religious devotion.

Pirina gazed wistfully at the image, as if he were an old sweetheart. "I inherited this from my mother. It is more than a hundred years old." She paused, then implored quietly, "When you are at the Church of San Lázaro, ask after my health. Ask on behalf of all Cubans, so that . . ." She stopped, shut her lips tightly, and said no more. I wanted to press. What did she want for all Cubans that she couldn't share with me—more freedoms? More beans in the monthly ration? The end of *el bloqueo*?—but she retreated as if she had already said too much, and I didn't push. I had learned to respect the silences that plopped unexpectedly into conversations, instinctively braking so as not to offend or force others to jeopardize their safety on my behalf. Conversational compromise felt like a small price to pay for being in a country I had come to love and which had embraced me and all my befuddlement.

I was finishing off slices of fresh pink papaya with lime when I heard Enrique call from the patio, "Sor Juanita!" His gentle mockery in calling me "Sister" made me smile self-consciously and feel the gap between my secular humanism and any form of organized religion. My parents had raised us as Presbyterians to give us a dose of the Judeo-Christian tradition, but they had been weak on follow-through. When we left home, they shifted their allegiance to the Unitarians while I turned to the Sunday *New York Times* and a cup of coffee.

Settling onto the worn upholstery of the passenger seat, I looked over at my friend, clean-shaven and wearing a fresh short-sleeved shirt. His face was haloed by his frizzy brown hair. "Ah, Juanita, in the next few days, you're going to see incredible things," he said, grinning impishly. "Are you ready?" He delighted in pushing my limits and for an instant I could see the boy in him.

"*¡Sí, lista!*" I answered, not wanting him to sense my trepidations. As he cranked the ignition and the engine turned over, his reassuring presence hit my system like a drug and I relaxed, giving myself over to the inevitability of whatever lay ahead.

We bounced along in the Moskovitch, crossing Vedado and heading toward the highway that lead to the airport. The seat felt familiar, as if the supporting coils had adjusted to my frequent presence. On each trip to Cuba I had seen new evidence of Enrique's latest skirmish with rust; new patches of sanded surface and fresh paint. Even as I tried to adjust myself to avoid the wiry poke of springs, I appreciated that this car—with all its uncomfortable idiosyncrasies—was as friendly and welcoming to me as its owner.

Bump, lurch, swerve, bump—it was sweltering as we made our way out of the city by way of the Plaza of the Revolution. We passed the Ministry of the Interior where the eyes of a gigantic face of Che Guevara in sculptural relief looked down on us. Curving around a bend and past the statue of José Martí, we turned south on a route familiar to me from my numerous arrivals and departures at the international airport.

The convent was located a dozen or so kilometers past the airport on the same highway; first the psychiatric hospital, then the airport, then the residential center for AIDS patients at Santiago de Las Vegas, and finally El Rincón, the leprosarium. Insanity, AIDS, and leprosy—everyone's worst fears, I thought—no wonder this was the favored route of pilgrims seeking God's favor in times of illness.

It was Havana hot and Enrique's Russian car had no air-conditioning. His attention was fixed on the road, patches of his shirt translucent with sweat. To avoid clouds of dust and diesel, he cranked up his window each time a car rolled by, cranking it down again when danger passed. The highway narrowed to a scant two lanes as we approached El Rincón. Flower sellers were setting up stalls at the entrance to the village. Purple and yellow blossoms peered out of cellophane wrappers next to plaster religious icons. A freshly painted outdoor café with a fenced off sitting area awaited its first customers. *"Divisa,"* Enrique commented, his eyes darting my way, expecting me to fill in what he didn't say. Dollars only. With limited access to hard currency, few Cubans would find refreshment there.

We slowed at the square park in front of the Church of San Lázaro. On our right stood the creamy edifice with its dark red roof, looking small relative to its renown. In the park, clusters of men, women, and children milled around. Brown patches of dirt showed where foot traffic had defeated grassy green. Although it was still three days before the eve of San Lázaro and the climactic culmination of the pilgrimage, people were already gathering on the steps that lead into the sanctuary. I scanned the crowd of early arrivals, expecting to see something unusual—a prostrate penitent whipping himself or a leprous person covered in sores—but noted nothing out of the ordinary.

Just beyond the church we approached the guard station of the leprosarium. Several scruffy old men with yellowed teeth sat on a wall to the left, talking to each other. One was shirtless, another missing a leg. Catching my breath I wondered what else awaited me on the grounds. We pulled up to the guard station, and with Enrique's mention of the mother superior we were waved through. A few hundred yards later we stopped in front of the convent where empty wrought iron chairs sat expectantly on the front portico.

Enrique leaned across the front seat from the driver's side to jiggle open the temperamental door on my side. I stepped out into the heat of the midday sun and felt a fresh rush of apprehension. A ring of the bell summoned a slender woman in street dress who opened the heavy wooden door and showed us into the front parlor. The sudden coolness of the high-ceilinged room was a welcome surprise.

Sor Carmen was expecting us. When she appeared, amiable and soft-spoken in a knee-length habit of beige and white, her presence calmed me. Her big brown eyes exuded kindness. She was closer to my daughter's age than my own, but I felt her presence as maternal nonetheless. We sat in wooden chairs and, as in our earlier visit months before, were served sugary *cafecitos* in tiny white cups. After the rituals of friendly greetings, she turned to Enrique. "One of the sisters told me she had heard that a *norteamericana* was coming to work with us in El Rincón," Sor Carmen said, her eyes quizzical and glancing in my direction, "even before I told them Juanita would be coming." She looked puzzled. "I can't be sure," she added, "but I imagine the word came from someone working for state security."

The mother superior's manner was casual but I didn't like what I was hearing. Was someone tracking me? The two old friends spoke quickly, consonants evaporating, my comprehension diminishing. Fear rose in my chest like mercury in a thermometer. I'd heard vague stories of foreigners being hassled and journalists being deported for crossing the often invisible lines of acceptable deportment.

"Look," Sor Carmen exclaimed suddenly, directing Enrique my way. "We've made her *muy nerviosa.*" I was both embarrassed and relieved at her recognition. She laughed and touched my arm gently. *"¡No se preocupe!"* she said, looking at me intently. "We live with this all the time."

But I didn't! This was totally out of my repertoire. At the thought of being followed, my pulse quickened. It was a prospect clearly beyond my limits for acceptable adventure. Suddenly I remembered that I had left my passport in Havana and wasn't carrying a copy. Since I had never been stopped and asked to show identification except at the health ministry, I had become casual about such matters. Should anyone require me to account for myself, a passport was the least I would need. But my fright went deeper than the fear of being followed or caught without a passport, burrowing back in time to Sputnik, childhood nightmares of "commie" invasions, and memories of crouching under my school desk during air raid drills. Communists were the Bad Guys. In the space of a few moments, the red menace of communism completely eclipsed other anxieties. Inside I was regressing at record speed, struggling not to think about being detained, interrogated, or worse.

"Mire," Sor Carmen said calmly, taking command of the situation. "Here's what you need to do to avoid trouble." I was ready to listen.

"Don't ask a lot of questions or do anything where you could be perceived as interviewing. You never know with whom you are talking. The town is full of workers for state security and *policía.*"

"Don't take notes when you are outside of the convent."

"Don't take pictures of the pilgrimage until you see a lot of other people taking pictures."

"Don't walk around the hospital by yourself."

Those were the rules and, although Sor Carmen assured me that nothing bad would happen, the fear of God was instilled—or the fear of the state—I couldn't tell the difference. I felt penitent, suppressing the urge to confess my impulses to talk freely with people and to take notes and pictures.

Enrique made ready to leave. I felt the tug of his impending departure as if I were about to lose the protection of a big brother. For an instant I thought about the laptop that hung from my shoulder. I had heard that departing travelers sometimes had computer discs and notes confiscated by *policía* at the airport. Who knew about convents? Impulsively I handed the computer to Enrique. Should a state official choose to question me, it would be safer at his house than with me. In giving over my most familiar and comforting companion, I was relinquishing the last relic of my academic identity.

Enrique slipped the strap over his shoulder. *"Sí, mejor,"* he said. Good idea. I searched his eyes. He didn't look worried. We embraced. His cheek was scratchy and moist as it brushed mine.

The convent complex, a century-old cement and stucco structure, capaciously housed a dozen sisters and a comparable number of permanent staff who washed clothes, tended the garden and the kitchen, and maintained the building. I was relieved to discover that the sisters had their own dining room and sleeping quarters. There were extra rooms for guests. Sor Carmen showed me mine, tucked in the back recesses of the convent and accessible either by walking through a central patio filled with flowering plants or by cutting through the kitchen and navigating a shadowy hallway past the sisters' quarters. In the bathroom off my room, a large crucifix complete with bleeding Jesus leaned against the wall next to a broom and a dirty mop. I took to crossing myself whenever I brushed my teeth.

My roommate was a buxom older woman named Silvia. She was from Regla, a poor municipality of Havana, and was one of dozens of volunteers who took up residence at the convent during the pilgrimage. These *Amigos de San Lázaro,* as they were called on the pinafores they wore, supplemented the year-round staff during the December festivities. At the church, the

Amigos received the offerings brought by the pilgrims. In the convent they prepared food, assisted in the laundry, and helped the sisters receive visitors.

That first evening, a grandmotherly sister with a sweet high-pitched voice offered me dinner from four steaming caldrons on the kitchen counter. I helped myself to soup, salad, and fried plantains and ate quietly at a table with Silvia and several other *Amigos.* After supper, Silvia offered to instruct me in convent bathing. Following her example, I filled a pail with hot water from the kitchen and lugged it to our private bathroom where—pleased to find a large new bar of soap—I scooped the water and dumped it over my head with a plastic bowl. This was exactly how I had bathed decades earlier in the Peace Corps, and the warm suds felt like a youthful baptism.

Cleansed and completely spent, I slipped into my nightgown. Before succumbing to the welcome of my bed, I forced myself to jot notes about the day in a small notebook, a poor substitute for my laptop but what I had at hand. The day's demands had exhausted me and I was too tired to ponder the unknowns of the days ahead. The cotton sheets on my bed were thicker and whiter than any I had seen in Cuba and as crisp as the night air. I pulled the covers around me, exquisitely aware that this experience was a gift, and slipped into the delicious oblivion of a baby's sleep.

My next awareness was of expanding warmth under my body, warmth that radiated out from where my hip met the mattress. Although my face was chilled, under the covers I was lulled by gentle heat, comforting me in the early morning hours. When the warmth turned to wetness and finally pierced my somnolence, it was already too late. My gown and the bed were soaked. For the first time in my adult life, I had wet the bed. The pungent scent of urine emanated outward, wafting transgression toward sisters and *policía* alike.

chapter 22

I didn't know what to expect in my convent stay, but waking up on the first day in a bed wet with urine wasn't in the plan. I was mortified, and confessing such a transgression to anyone who could exchange my sheets for fresh ones was beyond what I could fathom. Luckily I was alone. My roommate Silvia had already risen and left to assume her morning duties. I examined the size of the moist blotch. Not too bad. I blotted it with a damp towel and let the sheet air while I prepared for the day. Then I rearranged the linens and tucked the offensive portion under the mattress. My behavior was that of a five-year-old.

For the next four nights I positioned myself carefully when I went to bed, hoping to maintain strategic distance from any residue. Thankfully, I figured out the laundry system, and on my last day with the nuns, I stripped all of the linens, wrapped them discretely with my dirty towels and, with joyful relief, handed the bundle to the woman in charge.

If the sisters were clairvoyant or judgmental as I had imagined them to be, they didn't let on what they knew. Ironically, from the moment Sor Carmen alerted me to the possibility that I was being followed by state security, I experienced the sisters as close allies. They introduced themselves to me one by one as our paths crossed in the convent, and I tried to learn their names as best I could. There were about a dozen in all. Without the usual cues of dress and hairstyle, I had to study their features and voices carefully to sort out who was who. Their snug white wimples squeezed their cheeks and framed features that only sometimes distinguished one from another. In contrast, no one had trouble recognizing me—I was the only *norteamericana*, the only non-Catholic, and—I was sure—the only person who was working so hard to figure everything out as I went along.

Enrique had told Sor Carmen of my interest in health care, my position with a medical school, and my desire to observe the pilgrimage. I don't know what was passed on to the other sisters, but their welcome felt straightforward. They asked for no details and took me in as if naturally I should be among them. The most outgoing of the sisters was María Jesús, a handsome and voluble woman about my age with thick eyebrows, large frame glasses, and a fringe of black hair that poked out the edges of her wimple. She was in charge of collecting medicines and maintaining the convent dispensary and seemed always to be darting about the convent at hypo-manic speed. The supplies dispensed by the sisters came from international agencies, including various Catholic charities in the United States, and from foreign visitors like me. Hundreds of people from all over Cuba regularly came or sent emissaries to the convent in search of medicines not available at the state pharmacies.

I gave Sor María Jesús the surgical gloves, gauze, and other medical supplies that I had raided from a family medicine clinic at home. She gratefully accepted them and took me to see their hodge-podge of a dispensary. I examined the limited stock. Among boxes of antibiotics were a few cartons of the newer antidepressants not yet part of the Cuban pharmacopeia. Those available through local *consultorios* and the health ministry were old-fashioned by American standards; patients had to wait longer for the drugs to take effect and side effects were more problematic. Of the newer antidepressants, the sisters possessed only enough to treat one person for a few weeks.

A novitiate who hadn't yet taken her final vows was the loveliest and youngest of the group. Sor Isis was as beautiful as the Egyptian goddess of her name. Her thickly lashed eyes were sheltered by a Frida Kahlo brow, and her habit did nothing to diminish her sensual appeal. She was one of the few sisters not trained as a nurse, but she was responsible nevertheless for the daily cleaning and dressing of the leprous ulcers that plagued some of the patients. She looked angelic, and I imagined the men standing in line, the pain of wound debridement a small price to pay for the sweet comfort of her attentions.

Sor Pilar was the oddest, both in appearance and behavior. She was strikingly triangular, her wide base anchored with heavy black laced shoes, the point of her head defined by her wimple which she constantly removed, readjusted, and repositioned. She had but two top teeth, and her cheeks collapsed into her mouth when she spoke, making her all but unintelligible. While only in her sixties, she looked more elderly, with prominent eyes, a dowager's hump and bandages that migrated from one limb to another during my stay. *"Osteoporosis,"* she explained more than once, "*y dolor.*" Pain. She smiled, apparently pleased to be suffering. Sor Pilar frequently trailed me within the convent walls, popping up in unexpected places nattering in my direction with no apparent awareness of how little I could understand.

Older than Sor Pilar but younger in spirit was Sor Lázara, named for the saint whose miracles inspired the pilgrimage and blessed with a nurturing nature that drew everyone around her close. I wanted to sidle up to her for warmth and claim her as my *abuelita.* Her character suited her position in charge of the kitchen. With the help of a rowdy and friendly team of staff and *Amigos,* she prepared sustenance for us all, offered with a soft soprano voice that projected care far beyond the provision of food and drink.

I wondered what brought this extraordinary collection of strong women together as Sisters of Charity. Was it pure religious devotion or other callings had led them to vows of poverty and the care of the sick and pilgrims? I wondered if they wavered in their commitments; if, like me, they were prone to burn-out. Did middle-aged sisters become disillusioned with their religious order as I had become disillusioned with my academic order? Does everyone eventually ask, "Is this all there is?" and yearn for something more?

On Saturday morning, Sor Carmen asked me if I wanted to join her to make rounds among the patients, just the two of us. Since the leprosarium surrounded the convent, we reached our destination with a step off the front porch. We walked among the buildings and I could see major changes since my visit six months earlier. Several of the patient pavilions that had then been in ruins and unoccupied were barely recognizable, now freshly painted and pristine. The restored buildings contrasted starkly with the few that remained untouched by repairs and whose windows were covered with plywood.

Through the open door of a restored pavilion, I saw the shine of newly polished marble floors. Solar panels had been installed on the roof to provide hot water for new bathrooms. We climbed the steps to enter. The room was ample and airy. Sunlight streamed in through tall, shuttered windows. We walked down the middle aisle. Residents lounged about in twos and threes. Several sat in their rockers. Some wore pajamas, others T-shirts and pants. All suffered from leprosy. Some were missing limbs. I searched their faces and hands for signs of further deformity but to my relief and disappointment nothing obvious stood out.

Sor Carmen greeted every patient by name, touching each, a hug here, a pat on the head there. She buttoned the shirt of one, told another fellow in a bright blue cap that he looked *elegante*, and chided a youth whom she hadn't seen in chapel. Patients looked pleased to engage with her, if only for a minute or two. She introduced me to patients along the way, and I did my best to join in casual interaction, though being neither a sister nor a patient I felt self-conscious.

When we encountered laborers putting finishing touches on a bathroom, Sor Carmen's manner shifted and she briefly morphed into construction contractor, overseeing details of the ongoing renovations. I was impressed by the quality and scope of the work. "Did the government provide the funds for these changes?" I asked. After all, it was a state facility. "No," she replied. "The health ministry gave permission for the renovations but the funds came from the church, mostly from the offerings pilgrims bring to pay homage to San Lázaro." I was beginning to glimpse the close interrelationships of the pilgrimage, the Catholic Church, and this state medical facility.

Returning to the convent, I followed Sor Carmen's lead and scrubbed my hands vigorously with soap and water in the sink at the entrance to the sisters' quarters. Leprosy might not be easily contagious but I was taking no chances.

~

Over the days that I spent with the sisters, they approached me one by one, often initiating conversation about matters of health. I couldn't tell if the topic was in response to something Sor Carmen had told them or because health was among their primary concerns. The exception was Sor Pilar, who took delight in sharing a daily update of her health status, giving what doctors at home would call an "organ recital." She went so far as to show me the special concoction that she used to soothe her delicate skin. With private insurance in the United States she might have elicited thousands of dollars of work-up.

Sor María Jesús narrated the details of a recent minor stroke that had resulted in her falling and for which she was getting physical therapy. The doctors had told her that the transient ischemic attack was the result of serious osteoporosis and deterioration of her cervical spine, although she was just in her fifties. "I'm in a lot of pain," she said, her eyes wide with disbelief. "And I've been told that I must move very carefully." I would never have guessed the gravity of her problems from the speed with which she raced from one task to another. "There is no culture here that encourages women over forty to consume calcium," she said, exasperation showing. "And besides, it is very difficult to locate calcium pills." I thought of the population of Cuba, aging like our own. Calcium deficiencies in post-menopausal women might not put a major dent in their longevity statistics, just in the quality of life of thousands and thousands of women.

Listening to the sisters, I knew that I would always be interested in health and medicine and the mysterious domain where individual psychology meets the body. I had spent too many years as a clinical psychologist for it to be otherwise. Even so, by the time I reached the convent, my professed purpose as a health researcher had become secondary to what I wanted more: a fuller engagement in the nitty-gritty of human experience and a bigger bite of all that life had to offer. I wanted to know the strange richness of being a compound Other: a fallen Unitarian among Catholic sisters, a foreigner among Cubans, a relatively healthy person among patients with leprosy, an observer among pilgrims. And I was getting what I wanted, immersion in an alternate reality light-years distant from the predictable paradigms and pressured productivity that I knew too well.

chapter 23

the geography of my stay encompassed the convent, the leprosarium, the Church of San Lázaro and the surrounding village of El Rincón. Out of fear of what might happen otherwise, I conformed to the rules Sor Carmen had suggested upon my arrival. Since I had no specified responsibilities and everyone else was busy with theirs, I was on my own to structure my time. I alternated between walks to the church and village where I observed the progress of the pilgrimage and attended mass, and retreats to the convent where I compulsively noted my observations in an effort to document my research activities for OFAC. I discovered that writing detailed field notes from memory took discipline and I came to enjoy the practice. Spare hours when I wasn't eating or sleeping were spent helping the *Amigos* and kitchen staff in their culinary efforts to keep ahead of the rising tide of hungry pilgrims, priests, and visitors.

With time on my hands, I attended at least one mass each day, a rate of church attendance that would compensate for years of religious negligence and at least disguise my heathen status, if anyone cared. The frequency of services escalated in synchrony with the ever-increasing flow of pilgrims into the usually sleepy town.

The first afternoon, I attended a special service for sisters, patients, and guests that was held in the convent chapel. Students from the catechism class joined patients from the leprosarium to worship. As if to announce that all were welcome, one sick old man attended wearing his pajamas and carrying a catheter bag.

Two pre-pubescent children who looked like brother and sister saw me enter a pew by myself and scooted in, one on either side of me. Before the service began, the girl asked me to read the words of the hymns out loud. The three of us held the hymnal together and took turns reading. They stayed through the mass, stealing furtive glances at me. I couldn't tell if it was my imperfect Spanish, my blue eyes, or the way I fumbled through the service that held their interest. I was moved by their innocent impulse of inclusion.

After mass, Sor Carmen and Sor Ibis suggested that I accompany them to check on several couples who lived in the sixteen cottages of the sanatorium. I was pleased with their invitation because I'd been curious about the *matrimonios* ever since hearing of them. The *casitas* were located on the perimeter of the grounds in an area I had not seen. We walked three abreast down the narrow road of the leprosarium, passing pavilions where patients lingered on the steps talking with each other. They greeted us as we passed.

A low-flying airplane hummed loudly overhead and surprised us with a swoop. I tensed briefly in a moment of paranoia. Sor Carmen looked skyward at the plane and, spreading her arms wide, exclaimed for all to hear, "Take me away! Take me *anywhere*!" The two sisters doubled over in paroxysms of laughter barely constrained by their clerical garb.

Their outburst left me with questions I couldn't quite ask, a condition that was becoming chronic. From what exactly did she want to flee? The lives of the sisters looked appealing to me. They had a comfortable home, the satisfaction of meaningful work, and a close community. Sor Carmen had good food, no financial worries, and even a fancy new van at her disposal. I didn't know the source of her unrest, but I certainly recognized the urge to flee. Ironic that the very place she longed to leave behind was where I was finding reprieve.

At the end of a rough path of broken sidewalk we arrived at the threshold of the first of several cottages strung out in an arc under a scatter of shade trees. All were in need of repair and fresh paint, slated for the next round of renovation. Sor Carmen knocked on the door and the response was swift and friendly as an elderly Afro-Cuban couple answered and invited us in. Amidst a round of cheek kissing and handshakes, Sor Carmen introduced me as a convent guest. The man's knobbed fingers in mine made me think of the disease that had landed him in this place. His greeting was as cordial as if we knew each other well and visited regularly.

The sisters and leprosy patients displayed a palpable affection for each other and a comfortable openness toward me. I tried to follow their example, although against all rational judgment I still felt a bit squeamish about leprosy. Mostly I was afraid that just around the corner I might see disfigurement beyond what I could handle and be unable to disguise my discomfort. The couple showed no embarrassment about their condition and the sisters touched them freely. In this nook of the Cuban health care system, human relations appeared exemplary.

Sor Carmen asked the old man how he was getting along. *"No muy bien,"* he replied. His wife stood next to him looking worried as he lifted his navy blue shirt to reveal the bulge on his lean torso where he hurt. The mother superior patted his belly lightly. It was hard and he wasn't moving his bowels. Sor Carmen put her arm around his shoulder and looked at both of them with compassion. "I'll see what we can do," she said softly.

We left. With the cottage door closed behind us, Sor Carmen said that the gentleman probably had a malignant tumor. She wasn't sure and probably couldn't confirm her suspicion; there were ongoing difficulties getting X-rays because of broken equipment and film shortages at the hospital where patients were sent for tests. I marveled at her equanimity, her ability to continue to dispense loving care without any show of the feelings that welled up so readily in me: anger at my government for impeding access to sorely needed supplies.

I pondered the suffering that probably awaited the old man, unsure that he would suffer any less if he were a patient in an Ohio hospital. In Cuba, without a definitive diagnosis, he would be spared the slash and burn of modern cancer treatment. No surgery or chemotherapy or radiation would gamble his misery for unlikely cure. He would die among family and friends in the care of the Sisters of Charity. Still, it bothered me that, dependent as he was on the kindness of nuns as his only resource, he might have no choices to make about medical treatment in his final days.

At a second cottage, we were greeted by a sallow-faced couple with matching pug noses, the result of the deterioration of nasal cartilage from their shared disease. Their living room was a scream of color: hot pink curtains, green walls, and a rainbow-hued afghan draped over the back of a chair. At Sor Carmen's prompting, the woman of the house opened a dresser drawer and removed a stack of white bedspreads that she had crocheted with her leprosy-stumped fingers. Proudly she spread them out in front of me and smoothed them as best she could. Neither she nor her husband seemed self-conscious about their deformities. I asked if I could take a picture. They looked pleased and positioned themselves smiling in front of a photograph of themselves with Pope John Paul II, taken during his 1998 visit to the sanatorium.

~

Strolling with the sisters on the leprosarium grounds, I felt safer and more secure than when I was by myself in the village or the church. Beyond the leprosarium gate, I felt more vulnerable; the possibility that I was being watched always lingered at the edge of my consciousness. The awareness that I didn't have my passport with me heightened my apprehensions. I hadn't knowingly disobeyed any Cuban law, but that didn't seem to matter. At times I felt as guilty as if my nails were covered with tell-tale white marks and I was being dragged to the confessional for interrogation.

When I walked to the village I tried to keep a low profile, a feat I accomplished by heading for the most densely populated areas. Following Sor Carmen's advice, I never took notes in public nor did I engage in lengthy conversations with anyone. Instead, I observed intensely in an almost meditative state, trying to memorize sensory details and construct descriptions of people to record later. The exercise sharpened my perceptions.

Since my arrival in El Rincón four days ahead of the climax of the pilgrimage, penitents had been steadily coming into the town and to the church, the density increasing by the hour. Many modest one-story houses along the main street had spawned *negocios* to address their needs. Under a homemade tin awning, bouquets of cellophane-wrapped sunflowers stood tall in a row while a distracted young vendor bounced a girlfriend on his knee. Some stands sold *refrescos*, snacks of peanuts or fried dough, while others hawked religious icons, sloppily spray-painted in primary colors. S*antos* were for sale in both Catholic and *santería* incarnations: wood-carved San Lázaros mixed with plaster versions of Babalú Ayé and charms to ward off the evil eye.

Along the main street, dogs staked out their turf on roof tops, barking at pilgrims passing below. Most of the devoted looked as if they could have been drawn from the streets of Central Havana, simply dressed in blue jeans, cotton shirts or halter tops. A one-legged man struggled against the odds to ride a tricycle past a mother and daughter dressed in matching *santería* white. Another boy walked by in a T-shirt featuring a red, white, and blue map of the United States. I noticed many worn heels and shredded leather shoes. In the church sanctuary a woman in skin-tight scarlet top stood next to a sign that said "*Se prohíbe Lycra.*" Lycra was forbidden, a hopelessly doomed initiative of the ecclesiastical fashion police.

Most pilgrims arrived on foot, not just from nearby villages and from Havana, thirty kilometers away, but also from far reaches of the island. Some took weeks or months to make the journey. From who knows where, a barefoot man in a shirt of burlap—Biblical sackcloth—pushed a wooden cart carrying a life-sized San Lázaro draped in purple. A black overnight bag was tucked under his robes.

A crowd of walkers parted and I saw what I had previously only imagined. Face down in the grime of the road, a man was dragging himself forward with his arms. His sunburned back glistened with sweat, and he looked exhausted, as if he had traveled far too long. His movements were crablike; his hands clawed the ground, and his trunk twisted unnaturally as he thrust each arm forward and levered himself along on the insides of pants-torn knees. Just as Enrique had said, I was seeing things I had never even imagined, harbingers of more to come.

Few of the pilgrims looked obviously sick. Many looked tired. Some looked playful and relaxed, although moods seemed to shift toward seriousness as people closed in on the church hoping for moments of epiphany or blessing.

I paused near the entrance to the sanctuary where five or six men were gathered. Several had open sores on their legs and feet and held white and purple candles and wooden boxes to receive donations to San Lázaro. A few feet away, sitting on a broken curb next to a prosthetic leg that she had removed, a woman in rags collected alms. To look pathetic seemed to be a calling. I wondered how many people solicited offerings at this same spot every year and how often personal economic need trumped religious zeal and collections for the convent. At a fountain behind the church, a couple struggled to constrain their spastic child and anoint him with holy water.

When I had absorbed all I could or reached my limit of heat, dust, and dehydration, I wended my way back to the convent, wondering if before reaching the gate I would be stopped by the guard or noticed and queried by someone from state security. Sor María Jesús advised me that if questioned, I should claim to be a visiting nun. It was a dissimilation I knew I could never pull off.

The kitchen was in a constant frenzy of food preparation. Piles of produce, long counters, huge sinks, and industrial-sized pots and pans required lots of workers, and Sor Lázara welcomed me whenever I felt like pitching in. Working on food preparation or cleanup offered me a way to contribute to the complex web of church, convent, and leprosarium and relief from having to think about what to do next. After dealing with the commotion beyond the leprosarium gate, I sought the comfort of the kitchen where I could relax washing beans or drying cutlery.

The kitchen, with Sor Lázara in charge, was Mother. When she asked me, I peeled an entire bucket of garlic and scored and sliced enough cucumbers to make salad for ninety. Teaming with my roommate Silvia, I folded hundreds of cardboard boxes to be filled with hot food for the *Amigos* working long shifts at the church. I cleaned rice with Joséfa, who worked in the laundry, and her husband Máximo. They showed me how to sort through kilos of rice on a gray cloth-covered table to pick out the tiny stones and pieces of burlap that mingled with the grains. If we didn't do a good job, Joséfa warned, we would be eating "*arroz con saco*" like common laborers—rice with the burlap bag it comes in.

Although when I was within the convent walls I never worried about being the subject of surveillance, surprises were frequent enough to keep me on my toes. Once, as I hurried through the darkened kitchen on the way to my quarters, I was stopped dead by a back-lit eight-legged silhouette. On the steel counter stretched not one but two humongous hogs, frozen solid, hooves pointing skyward and chests splayed open. I concluded we would soon be eating pork.

I often shared the kitchen with Sor Lázara's nephew Raul. He was a slender and handsome young man of Spanish origin who had travelled from Havana to volunteer his services during the rush. He was as kind as his aunt.

On Sunday afternoon, he was hard at work. The Cardinal of Cuba would be coming on Monday to dedicate one of the restored patient pavilions, and Raul was preparing a special meal that would be served to the sisters and their honored guest. For dessert he had little to work with. Following his instructions I helped him whip egg whites by hand to make meringues. As the clear slurry expanded into white froth with our efforts, he told me that he had learned gourmet cooking while working for Mexican and Canadian employers. More recently he had worked as a custodian at a foreign embassy but had been laid off, pending review of his political qualifications.

I couldn't imagine Raul as a custodian, let alone losing such a menial job for falling short on communist credentials. He was so bright, articulate, and well read, with impeccable social skills and a flair for food, that it was easier to imagine him as a diplomat. I wanted to know more about whatever had precipitated the loss of his job but hesitated to ask, never sure of the etiquette of inquiry in a country where open dissent incurred risks beyond my comprehension. Instead I diverted the conversation to matters of cuisine.

"Isn't the lack of ingredients frustrating?" I asked.

"Yes, of course. And you do need the proper conditions to prepare food." In characteristic good humor, he added, "Dealing with limits leads one to a larger spirituality." I shook my head and laughed. He had mastered the Zen of Cuban cooking.

I felt more at ease with the sisters than I ever anticipated that I would. The religion that bound them together was less salient to me than their shared ethic of service. I enjoyed the dominance of women behind the convent walls and appreciated the respect with which the sisters were treated by the male *Amigos* and the visiting priests. I especially enjoyed Sor Lázara, whose presence felt like being cuddled in a soft lap.

"If I were a Cuban," I said to her, musing out loud as we worked on dinner, "I think I'd want to become a sister and live with you all."

Her hands stilled from their task of cutting vegetables and she looked at me. "You don't have to be a Cuban to be a sister," she stated, her voice dancing in the upper octaves.

"I know," I replied, "but I have a husband."

Her eyes brightened. "Then you could become one when he dies!"

For an instant, that seemed possible.

~

Passing through the hall by the sisters' quarters, I heard tinkling, like rain on a tin roof, emanating from the crack of a barely open door. I couldn't imagine what it was. Unable to resist a peek, I poked my nose in the crack. A circle of sisters wearing latex gloves sat around a large table, their hands busily sorting through huge silvery mounds of coins that clinked in collective heavenly chorus.

I didn't know what to make of what I saw, but when one of them looked up to see me, I was aghast with embarrassment. I mumbled an apology and darted to my room, the unexpected scene reverberating in my mind. Suddenly I understood what the male *Amigos* were doing when they pushed heavy wooden boxes with hand-trucks from the church to the convent. They were moving voluminous offerings from church to convent, the donations that funded the renovations and supplemented state support of the leprosy patients.

The latex gloves that the sisters were using as they sorted the donations had not escaped my attention. I assumed they were those I had given them. When I next saw Sor Carmen, she looked chagrined and was compelled to offer explanation. "We have to wear gloves or we couldn't sort money," she said defensively. "It's too dirty and sticky. The alms come covered with tobacco, urine—everything!"

"No se preocupe," I assured, my turn to use the expression so often directed at me. Having seen the renovations that resulted from their labors, I was pleased to be an accomplice and relieved that she didn't scold me for my curiosity. Sor Carmen also seemed relieved. Like me, she didn't want to leave the wrong impression. Like me, she wanted her motivations to be perceived as legitimate.

One evening, as I walked past the sisters' dining room on the way to my room, Sor Carmen rose from the large table where she was eating with the other sisters and called to me. "I want you to meet someone," she said, then introduced me to Sor Mercedes, a visiting social worker with a Mayan round face and eyes that spoke of wisdom and experience. "Make arrangements to talk to each other," Sor Carmen suggested. "Sister Mercedes will answer any questions that you may have."

The following afternoon Sor Mercedes and I sat on iron chairs in the shade of the front porch and spoke, while patients, sisters, and *Amigos* passed by on their way to and from the leprosarium gate and the church beyond. With high cheekbones and the delicate fine lines of an aging face, she was beautiful, and her Spanish was utterly lucid, as if she were specially trained to communicate with foreigners.

From Sor Carmen's introduction, I didn't know what I was expected to ask her about—sisters, patients, pilgrims, or health care, so I just asked her what she did. Sor Mercedes' religious calling was to serve poor families in Havana and those with family members in prison. She lived in Havana and saw her mission there and in El Rincón during the pilgrimage as one of offering hope to people facing serious problems of hunger, need, and despair. In cases of extreme hardship, she tried to offer people concrete assistance in the form of food or clothing. "First they have to feel like human beings," she said, her voice deep and sonorous. "Only then you can talk to them about hope." Listening to her, I found her very presence reassuring. She was as grounded as an old tree with roots deep in the earth.

She continued, lamenting what she saw as worsening social conditions that made her work more difficult. "Sometimes people come to me and say, 'Sister, I *have* no hope, no hope for *anything*.'" She paused, searching for the right example. "I know a woman who had only one pair of bloomers that she had to wash out every night," she said. I thought of the panties with blue stars and pink hearts that were stuffed in a corner of my suitcase and knew they were destined for Sor Mercedes.

Our conversation shifted to the pilgrimage. "Some people come to San Lázaro to give thanks for blessings they have already received from God, others to ask for help in desperate situations," she said. "Many make the journey again and again, always asking, always needing, not just in December but every month."

"How can you tell which are which?" I asked. "Who is asking for help and who is giving thanks?"

"By their faces," she replied. "Look at their faces. Those asking for help—you can see it in their eyes."

chapter 24

From the kitchen where I was drying dishes with Raul, I could see across the patio to where a jovial group of women sat scraping clumps of dirt from yucca and peeling them for cooking. Several were *Amigas* whom I had already met. When I finished, I joined them. The women expanded their circle to make a space for me and handed me a knife and a bulb of yucca red with the clay that clung to it. I shook off the dirt as best I could and endeavored to strip the tough outer layers of the waxy tuber with a knife, as I had seen them do. It was harder than I thought, not at all like peeling potatoes.

Satisfied when I finished one, I followed the example of the woman next to me and washed it off in a tub of water. The bits of red mud looked like blood as they dispersed. Then I added my contributions to the accumulating pile of root which one of the women carried to the kitchen. A few minutes later she returned with yucca in both hands. Laughing, she passed them back to me: they were the ones I had prepared, rejected by the kitchen as inadequately peeled.

The joke was on me and the women enjoyed it, vying with each other to show me how to remediate. I needed to cut a bit deeper, make the peelings more uniform. As we worked, our hands, the knives, the table, and even the freshly-cut white tubers were smeared with the sticky red clay. I liked the feel of the muck in my fingers, the sense of simple common purpose, the easy generosity of women literally offering me their helping hands.

Wielding knives against the leathery outer layers, the women commented about the harsh effects of the sun on their skin and the harsh effects of the economy on their daily lives. *"Quien come no se veste. Quien compra ropa no come,"* one of them exclaimed, with a sigh. He who eats doesn't dress. He who buys clothes doesn't eat.

Guadalupe, an *Amiga* whose daughter was seeking permission to leave Cuba to join her husband in Florida, spoke of the vagaries of *el bomba*, the annual lottery Cubans enter for the chance to emigrate. Her daughter had applied and was waiting to hear. Guadalupe's voice cracked when she spoke of the possibility of separation from her only child. If she emigrated, further contact between them would be governed by the fickle and ever-changing regulations that controlled human relations across the Florida Straits. Guadalupe and her daughter wouldn't be able to count on what I took for granted: as long as I wasn't living in Cuba the distance between my daughter Karin and me could be vaporized with a credit card and an airplane ticket.

The love for our children completed our circle as we finished readying heaps of yucca for the mouths of our convent family.

~

It was Sunday evening and the next day would bring the final crescendo of pilgrims to El Rincón. Already trickles of penitents had become streams and then rivers, and the plaza in front of the church was a flood of congestion. More and more pilgrims were arriving, not just on foot, but on knees and bottoms, dragging themselves with their arms, and pushing their bare heels into the dirty road. I puzzled about what synergy of desperation, need, hope, and contrition would compel me to journey, naked-kneed, kilometer after kilometer along a hot and gravelly road. Only by fixing my mind on the people I loved and imagining them mortally ill and dependent on my acts of devotion could I begin to fathom their motives.

My pilgrimage paled by comparison. "To learn about health care in Cuba"—that had been the official mission that drew me to this most contradictory of countries, a mission that now felt hollow and distant against the intensity of my experience. "Quest" fit better than "pilgrimage" since my journeying had been fueled by secular angst rather than religious belief. Mine had been a quest to shake off—if only temporarily—the roles and expectations of home in order to just *be.* I had longed to dive into boundless waters beneath the warm top layer of the known and, like an aquatic explorer, poke into caves and paddle through plankton with the hope of being surprised—but not too surprised—by the next big fish. I had yearned to be startled into another kind of living, one in which the words "relish" and "delight" had more play than "trudge" and "duty."

I was beginning to understand that—as legitimate as they were in their own right—my apprehensions about state surveillance in Cuba and OFAC prosecution in the United States were proxies for other fears, fears of gambling the safety of my nailed-down life for something more.

On Monday morning, the day leading up to the climactic midnight service that ushered in the Fiesta of San Lázaro, I walked the dusty road to the church filled with a sense of homage to those who had helped me slip loose from my moorings. There was Gary who showed me what vital engagement looked like in old age and who kept asking me why I was in Cuba *really.* I wanted to claim his spirit as my own. There was Enrique, who kept throwing doors open just ahead of where I was. There was Phil at home—and my parents too—all so generously supportive of my travels. Between my Cuba jaunts, my father had said, "I'm not going to worry about you," conveying confidence that bolstered me when mine flagged. And my mother had said, "You're doing exactly what I wish I could do," her tone expressing more permission than envy. Her propensity for taking every advantage of serendipity had given me a template to follow when my first plans fizzled. And there were Sor Carmen and the sisters, *my* sisters, whose welcome reminded me that shared womanhood and shared humanity can transcend differences that might otherwise divide.

I felt prayerful, wanting to honor people everywhere who crave more adventure in their lives, who yearn to discover their own boundaries rather than accept the limits of convention and expectation, and who long to expend themselves utterly before they die. In honoring my own desires, I hoped that I was staking a claim that would encourage my daughter to pursue her own most fulfilling life.

~

The convent phone stopped working on Monday as the eve of the pilgrimage approached. The sisters weren't surprised, surmising that it was probably interference from state security. The same explanation was offered for the small planes that zipped low across the skies. Presumably the state was monitoring the crowds and looking for suspicious activity such as dissidents gathering amidst the hordes and violating laws against political assembly. I remembered Sor Carmen's comment, "We live with this all the time." Government surveillance was a routine that didn't ruffle the sisters, whose attentions were focused on more pressing matters: feeding pilgrims, responding to the barrage of requests for medicine, preparing the pavilions and patients for the Cardinal's visit, making sure that everyone who wanted to could attend mass and receive blessings from one priest or another.

The pilgrimage itself was tolerated but not encouraged by the state. In the early years after the revolution, the new government attempted to suppress the yearly ritual. The numbers of pilgrims diminished but they never stopped coming; instead of publicly proceeding along the main road from Havana to El Rincón, pilgrims took more clandestine routes, cutting through the fields that surrounded the village. Belief in the healing power of this pilgrimage was deeply engrained in the collective unconscious of Cuba.

Since the Pope's visit to Cuba, religious freedom and tolerance of *santería* traditions had increased, but I sensed that the truce between church and state was an uneasy one. In spite of the fact that the pilgrimage represented the largest display of religious fervor on the Cuban calendar, in Havana I had heard no mention of it on the state-run television.

As the bake of the rising sun replaced the chill of early morning, I walked to the village with Sor María Jesús, wanting to see for myself the building bustle of activity beyond the leprosarium. We walked past the dollars-only refreshment stand, almost empty, while people mingled in nearby doorways and porches of private homes, conversing with their friends and sipping sodas purchased with pesos. The peso stands that had sprung up overnight to address the needs of the peregrination were doing brisk business. Plastic chairs appeared on rooftops for family and friends wanting front-row seats for the events of the day.

Sor María Jesús gestured toward a cluster of young men in dark shirts and jackets relaxing under a shade tree. "Those are state security workers," she whispered. In their plain clothes, I wouldn't have known. They supplemented the uniformed provincial *policía* who stood out prominently in twos and threes scattered among the crowds. It occurred to me that maybe one of them had been assigned to keep an eye on me, but the thought no longer unsettled me.

We kept alert so as not to block the ever-thickening flow of pilgrims. One in particular grabbed my attention, a scraggly-looking woman sitting in the dirt and pushing herself backwards toward the church with the heels of her hands. She looked dehydrated and sunburned. From a rope tied around her wrist she dragged a plastic box that sheltered a plaster San Lázaro in his blue and white robes. From a heavy metal chain that encircled her left leg she dragged a large and lumpy block of cement, a demonstration of her pious suffering. She plowed a dusty trail as she awkwardly lugged herself along.

Sor María Jesús caught me staring. She leaned toward me, responding as if I had made an accusation. "The church doesn't ask her to do this," she said. "Such displays are entirely a matter of personal choice." I nodded, momentarily unable to find the Spanish I needed to convey that I wasn't offended, just amazed.

The throngs of pilgrims increased over the course of the day and over my successive walks from convent to town. The church inhaled and exhaled swells of believers in a string of celebratory masses. Sor Carmen said that the population would peak during the 10:30 evening mass that extended through midnight and announced *el Día de San Lázaro.* In past years as many as 50,000 people had pressed their way into El Rincón for the occasion.

Some pilgrims came by themselves carrying flowers, candles, or painted plastic or wood images of their beloved San Lázaro. Others came in small family groups or with friends. Most were on foot, but every few minutes I saw another pilgrim struggling along the gravelly road on tender knees or back or belly. They rivaled each other in acts of postural contrition.

"*Arrastrarse*" was my new verb—to drag oneself. The sister pointed to the back of the church where artifacts of rock and cement were piled high against a fence, the weighty residue of previous years and an ever-enlarging tribute to piety and hope. Each new pilgrim, *arrastrándose* to the church, drew my attention and that of Cuban bystanders too. We watched transfixed, as if sighting exotic birds or beached whales. I occasionally snapped a picture but observation alone made me more comfortable and allowed me to feel part of the sacred festivities rather than separated by a camera lens. I savored what my senses took in: a *santería* priestess spreading her tools of divination in front of a woman in an Ohio T-shirt while Red Cross workers conversed in the foreground and black-shirted state security workers looked on from behind.

Evening approached and the sky dimmed. The pungent smell of burning candle wax spiced the cold night air. Stars pierced the blackening sky. The atmosphere became charged with urgency as cold and exhausted pilgrims struggled to make it to the church in time for the culminating mass that would hurl them over the midnight hour.

Everywhere I turned there was drama. A young boy walked backward toward the church, bent over and sweeping the street clean ahead of his father who dragged himself along on his back, elbows bleeding and balancing another son on his knees. In the streets men and women pulling blocks of cement with their limbs wriggled forward, intermingled with people arriving on bicycles and in horse-drawn wagons. A young pilgrim in torn shorts and torn shirt scuffled forward on his knees. A placid brown dog was wrapped around his neck like a scarf, providing furry heat. With one hand the man held the pet's paws closely against his chest.

A bent woman brushed the street behind her with a makeshift broom of palm fronds. She cleared the path for a man who inched along on his back, supported on his elbows and buttocks. He held yellow gladiolas in one hand, a lit candle in the other, and a cigar in his mouth. In the dusk of early evening, the fragrance of hot wax mingled with tobacco smoke and the scent of flowers.

Another woman crawled by in the dirt, looking as scrawny and sad as one of the stray dogs I had seen in the sanctuary. *"¡Descanse!"* A woman's voice called to her through the night. Rest! The pilgrim obeyed and put her head down, motionless. When she looked up again she could see the church ahead amidst golden flickers of candlelight. If she could make it another hundred yards, her journey would be complete. To discharge her vows, she would pull herself up the stone stairs on her arms, writhe her way through the mob at the church doors, and drag herself to the altar rail where she would receive the priest's blessing.

Near the church entrance an ambulance waited, ready for any exigency. Red Cross workers stood close by, surveying pilgrims as they approached. A long-faced man in his twenties with a red and white *Cruz Rojo* patch on his sleeve leaned over a bare-chested man lying supine in the soil with eyes closed.

"¿Cómo estás?" the worker asked respectfully. Are you okay? He leaned over his patient, handling his arm gently and attaching a blood pressure cuff to assess his condition. The man's eyes opened but he didn't respond. His gaze was trancelike.

"Would you like some water?" he was asked. The penitent finally looked up, took sips from a cup while the Red Cross worker held his head, and then resumed wriggling forward on his buttocks.

It was nearing midnight and I wanted to get inside the church before the celebratory mass began. I tried to push my way through the throng to reach the main portals, but as I put my foot on the first step, the press of the mob lifted me off the ground. I was not moving of my own volition but as one cell of a much larger organism whose wisdom I had no choice but to trust. The swaying back and forth over which I had not an iota of control was at once exhilarating and terrifying. I willed myself to stay vertical, and a few long seconds later my feet found the ground at the top of the steps.

The sanctuary compressed the crowd to a density far beyond what any United States fire code would permit. I looked around. Exiting would be impossible if it suddenly became necessary. Pilgrims had claimed space by lighting candles and affixing them to the marble floor with globs of wax. Dogs like those that accompanied San Lázaro and licked his wounds wandered under thickets of feet. Raw eggs used in *santería* rituals mixed with cigar ashes on the floor. It seemed like the church could contain not a person more, and still they kept coming—dragging themselves, crawling on their knees and on their backs, perilously vulnerable should the assemblage get out of hand.

A priest stationed just inside the entrance greeted each pilgrim and tried to direct the hordes with his arms. "Let the pilgrim pass and complete his promise!" he called out. A seam opened and prostrate pilgrims moved forward in procession. A second priest waited at the altar, ready to reach out his hand in blessing while sisters and *Amigos* stood nearby accepting offerings. I saw Silvia in the crowd and several of her *Amiga compañeras.* Dressed in white pinafores and protected from the human deluge by a wooden rail, they were gathering alms in front of the statue of San Lázaro: coins, cigars, flowers, candles, even bottles of cooking oil, durable offerings that would be conveyed to the sisters for the sustenance of the leprosarium for the coming year.

Towering piles of yellow, white, and purple flowers quickly obliterated the view of the saint as one pilgrim after another added to the mounds. A teenager in a Crimson Tide T-shirt passed a handful of coins across the rail. Nearby a pair of twins wearing matching burlap shorts and berets stood in quiet prayer.

From the altar a priest led the congregation in a chant, *"Donde está Dios, nada le falta."* Where God is present, nothing is lacking. But as I looked at people's faces and in their eyes, I could see the lacking—the desperation that Sor Mercedes had told me I would see.

My long skirt brushed dangerously close to flaming candles that seemed to be everywhere that feet weren't. The crush of people and the din of voices made it harder and harder for me to catch the details of the scene. Out of the corner of my eye, I caught the familiar face of one of the sisters. Seeing me, Sor Aida pushed her way toward me and the crowd parted for her. She grabbed my arm and suggested we climb to the balcony over the nave to watch the scene from above. I followed her to a gate at the back of the sanctuary. It was locked and zealously guarded by an *Amigo* who let us enter then latched it behind us. We ascended the stairs.

At the top there were just three of us: Sor Aida, me, and a man in a University of Michigan Wolverines T-shirt who wielded a huge video camera aimed at the swirl of color and candlelight below. One of the priests had pointed him out to me earlier. "State security," he had said. I stood at the rail of the balcony flanked by sister and camera man: Church and State. With a mix of awe and contentment, I looked down on the spectacle as pilgrim after pilgrim pushed forward to the altar to receive the priest's blessing. Strange as it was, in this intense and peculiar maelstrom, I felt at peace. The drama was large enough to miraculously envelop us all, as wave after wave of pilgrims culminated their sacred journeys of struggle, perseverance, blessing, and release.

epilogue

White puffs of cumulus race across the blue summer sky. Tall pines dance and sway against each other in the windy gusts, and wrens flit back and forth between the bird feeder and the green of nearby bushes. Since leaving the university five years ago, this view has become as familiar and comforting to me as an old friend.

"Windows," I had said to the architect. "I want windows and light." After Havana I would have no less. He listened and helped me create a home office that encompasses both an intimate sitting area where I see psychotherapy clients and a long writing desk where I now sip coffee and gaze out through a wall of glass. The other day a deer wandered into the flower beds to graze, and I had to rush out to shoo her away. I count on the infinite distractions that these windows provide to remind me that the world is vast and ever-changing and that I occupy but a miniscule place in the scheme of things.

I wish I could say that I returned from Cuba and immediately quit my job, unwilling to spend another minute in confinement, but that's not what happened. In fact I hung on for another two and a half years, long after having psychologically abandoned ship, until I had logged just enough weeks, months, and years to warrant a decent state pension. Then I bailed. I'm not proud of purposefully lingering, but economic considerations were real and it took time to figure out how I would translate a bigger life in Cuba to a bigger life at home.

I wish I could say that the restrictions that impede travel to Cuba have eased since the events described in this book, but that's not true either. In 2003 President Bush eliminated people-to-people exchanges such as the one that first introduced me to the island. In 2004 he went further, tightening restrictions on educational trips and effectively eliminating over 90% of the college and university programs about Cuba that included in-country experience. Religious and humanitarian licenses, while still available, were severely curtailed and more easily attained by conservative organizations than progressive ones. Most egregious of all were tightened restrictions on travel by Cuban Americans to visit their family members on the island. Under Bush, such visits were restricted to once every three years without humanitarian exception, and "family" was narrowly and ethnocentrically defined.

Early in his administration, President Obama eliminated the restrictions on travel by Cuban Americans visiting family, and hopefully he will do more on behalf of "purposeful" travel. However to lift the travel ban altogether and dismantle the embargo requires congressional action. As of this writing, with the exception of family travel, all of the restrictions put into place by the Bush administration still stand as does the embargo. Ordinary citizens of the United States can legally travel to Baghdad, Seoul, or Timbuktu, but not to Havana.

Now buried under shards of experience is the faint memory of what I initially imagined I would accomplish in Cuba. My conscious intent had been to conduct research on health care and the effects of the embargo. In my grandiosity, I imagined that Cuba would welcome me to do this work, and that I would author a tome that would make readers swoon over the inhumanity of our government. But Cuba required engagement on its own terms.

In the end, though my research methods were unconventional, I learned enough to draw some conclusions. They are these: I believe that Cubans are justifiably proud of the universal access to primary care medicine that their country has achieved, of the emphasis placed on prevention and community education, and of the dedication of their physicians to service, both at home and abroad. I believe that the high aspirations of their state-controlled system have been unevenly actualized, in part because of scarcities in pharmaceuticals and medical supplies. In the face of want, Cuban doctors struggle to maintain morale and to meet the needs of their patients, and along with everyone else they struggle for their economic survival. Regarding matters of health—as in every other arena of Cuban daily life—*no es fácil.*

The World Health Organization reports longevity and infant mortality statistics for Cuba roughly equivalent to those of the United States. For a resource-poor country contending with a half century of economic embargo, this is no small accomplishment. The achievements of the Cuban health care system powerfully demonstrate what can be accomplished when governmental will to provide basic health care is strong and fiscal emphasis is placed on public health rather than profit. I believe that, without *el bloqueo*, Cuba could achieve even more, and that our country is morally implicated in the unnecessary suffering of the Cuban people.

The medical systems of both of our countries espouse the value of addressing the health needs of the community, but in the United States, a disease orientation and a narrow definition of who is "the patient" trump substantial commitment to education and prevention beyond the walls of clinics and hospitals. Physicians are financially rewarded for attending to those with insurance or means and for doing procedures—colonoscopies and surgeries—rather than talking with patients; and vast numbers of our population are excluded from any "community" served by our medical system. In contrast, "the patient" served by the Cuban system is the population of the whole country, and since their health professionals receive only meager incentives and no one is drawn to medicine by the prospect of wealth, the call to serve moves to center stage.

An email from Félix reminds me of the April afternoon when I accompanied him visiting patients in Cerro, his *tarjetas* for tracking home visits tucked neatly in his pocket. There had been no charges to these families for his care. No requirements to document pathology or find someone ill in order to justify stopping by and checking on them. No thought that pausing in the park to appreciate an old woman's recitation of a poem by Nicolás Guillen was anything other than the appropriate response of a healer.

If I were poor or my health afflictions minor, I would prefer to be a patient in Cuba, where I would be assured access to care, likely by a doctor who lived nearby, knew me well, and focused on community education and prevention. However, if I were seriously ill and financially well off, I'd rather be a patient in the United States, where high-tech medicine and high-cost pharmaceuticals would be within my reach. But with ambivalence; while our primary care practitioners and medical texts extol the importance of a personal doctor-patient relationship and "longitudinal, comprehensive, and coordinated care," few patients describe their experiences as approximating such ideals. The concept of "care" itself is endangered.

~

In my post-university life, activism on behalf of U.S.-Cuba relations has claimed some of my energies. I've discovered that giving fuller voice to my values and political opinions beats keeping them under wraps and taking antidepressants. The side-effects are better too: new networks of colleagues and friends, opportunities for travel, and the pleasures of shared purpose. My now-eight trips to Cuba have only intensified my conviction that we need more international exchanges rather than fewer, porous boundaries between countries rather than impenetrable ones. How else will we learn from each other? How else will we more fully comprehend that we are all just folks?

I keep returning to Cuba, almost against my will. Havana is ever cacophonous and steamy hot and the noxious diesel fumes haven't gone away, but I have "family" there now, and history. Always another hook snags me into grappling yet again with the OFAC regulations. Most recently it was an invitation to write a book chapter about the practice of clinical psychology in Cuba. I passed days sitting in uncomfortable hotel lobby chairs in meetings with impassioned psychologist colleagues. While they shared their perspectives on Marx and Vgotsky and the importance of thinking about psychological problems in socio-historical context, I was distracted by furniture fantasies, wondering why finding a chair in an old Havana hotel that neither swallowed nor poked me should be so elusive. Such exasperating peculiarities are paradoxically part of what keeps drawing me back.

Yes, the chapter on Cuban psychology was for an academic text. In my reconfigured life, I may have left the university behind but I will always be—in part—my father's daughter. Still, I have claimed the luxurious right to say yea or nay to projects that invite my involvement and to favor those that express whole swaths of self which lay dormant or dying before my sabbatical flight. It's not easy. I ruminate about choices—about what constitutes a meaningful investment of all that one is. And I'm ever dogged by the awareness that there's no time to squander.

By the cusp of middle age, every sentient human being has become a unique and precious amalgam of skills, passions, knowledge, and experience. I believe that we are meant to be spent and that the world needs our most lavish gifts. Whether the yearning to exhaust all accounts before merging with the cosmic soup is universal or just hounding me, I don't know, but I'm looking to spree.